PIANO SONATA NO. 2 CONCORD

WITH THE ESSAYS BEFORE A SONATA

CHARLES IVES

Introduction by
Stephen Drury

DOVER PUBLICATIONS, INC.
Mineola, New York

Copyright

Copyright © 2012 by Dover Publications, Inc.
Introduction © 2012 by Stephen Drury.
All rights reserved.

Bibliographical Note

This Dover edition, first published in 2012, is an unabridged republication of *Essays Before a Sonata*, 1920, and Piano Sonata No. 2, *Concord*, 1922, originally published by the Knickerbocker Press, New York. Stephen Drury has prepared a new Introduction specially for this Dover edition.

International Standard Book Number

ISBN-13: 978-0-486-48863-9
ISBN-10: 0-486-48863-2

Manufactured in the United States by Courier Corporation
48863202   2013
www.doverpublications.com

INTRODUCTION

This sonata is exceptionally great music—it is, indeed, the greatest music composed by an American, and the most deeply and essentially American in impulse and implication.
—Lawrence Gilman, 1939

And many, including this writer, would say that it still is. *Concord* looms over the firmament of twentieth-century composition—not only music by American composers, not only music for the keyboard, but over the whole realm of concert music experience. Ives would have been the first to deny the possibility of a single "greatest" piece of music, but it is extremely difficult to refute the power that *Concord* exerts over both listener and performer. Ives' imagination, compositional technique, and spiritual vision come together to create an impact which is unique and unprecedented. Certainly *Concord* finds its place comfortably alongside Schoenberg's *Moses und Aron*, Stravinsky's *Rite of Spring*, Cage's *Renga with Apartment House 1776*, and Reich's *Music for Eighteen Musicians*, not to mention Ives' own Fourth Symphony (so intimately related to *Concord* through the second movements of each work, as well as general structural outlines and metaphysics).

I

Born in Danbury, Connecticut, in 1874, Ives studied piano and various other instruments early on, specializing in the organ, and started creating his own compositions in his early teens. The strongest single influence on Charles Ives' musical aesthetic was his father—bandmaster, church and theater musician, and music teacher. George Ives was a famous bandmaster during the Civil War before returning to Danbury. He transmitted a love and respect for a wide variety of music to his son, including European concert ("classical") music, as well as hymns, marches, popular songs of the day and other vernacular styles (such as ragtime, which was developing in popularity during Charles' college years). Along with this ecumenical attitude and the discipline of music making (both performing and composing), George also showed by example the necessity of invention, literally and figuratively. Making machines to play in quarter-tones, struggling to imitate the sound of church bells on the piano, playing "Swanee River" in one key while singing it in another—stories which Charles cites in reference to his father's musical activities—all these place George Ives alongside Thomas Edison and Alexander Graham Bell in the American inventor tradition. In a sense, Charles would go on to invent concert music in the New World: a new kind of concert music, a concert music beyond concert halls, as open to the sounds of life as a marching band or music in the park, but with a reach not limited by time or place.

Ives attended Yale College, majoring in music and studying composition with Horatio Parker, a highly trained (in Germany), conservative, strict, and accomplished composer and teacher. The young composer's urge to experiment was counterbalanced by Parker's formal and traditional approach. These two influences, the experimental and the formal, shaped Ives' mature music, and position him as a central (although unknown in his time) transition figure between the end of the Romantic era and the great explosion of sound which marks twentieth-century Western music. Like Beethoven, Ives was able to see into the past and future simultaneously, combining that archetypical 19th-century form the tone poem with what would become the new century's contribution to the history of form, collage. Also like Beethoven, Ives would come to the point in his trajectory as a composer where he would reach back even more deeply into musical history. For Beethoven it was the fugue, for Ives, the large-scale, multi-movement instrumental sonata.

It was early in his college years when Charles' father died. Ives felt this devastating loss for the rest of his life; the memory of his father and the emotional impact of his absence resonate throughout Ives' most personal music, his songs and piano sonatas. (The wistful figure that winds through and eventually concludes the First Sonata is an unfinished fragment of a phrase his father would sing while saying grace before a meal.) In his writing about the "Thoreau" movement in *Essays Before a Sonata*, the composer allows himself an emotional outburst:

> *You, James Russell Lowells! You, Robert Louis Stevensons! You, Mark Van Dorens! with your literary perception, your power of illumination, your brilliancy of expression, yea and with your love of sincerity, you know your Thoreau, but not my Thoreau—that reassuring and true friend, who stood by me one "low" day, when the sun had gone down, long, long before sunset.*

After Yale, Ives attempted to establish himself as a professional musician and composer, working as organist and choir director in churches in New Jersey and Manhattan, and producing a large-scale cantata (within a fairly conservative musical language), while keeping body and soul together clerking at an insurance company. A review of the cantata, *The Celestial Country*, survives with Ives' handwritten scrawl over the top: "Damn rot and worse." Ives determined that he would be unable to pursue his own muse within the conservative American musical establishment, left behind the professional music world, and went on to become one of the country's leading insurance executives, helping to revolutionize the industry. In near total isolation from the musical community, Ives worked furiously nights and weekends, and while commuting to and from work, created one of the great bodies of concert music, ultimately including four symphonies, two piano sonatas, four violin sonatas, over one hundred songs, and other choral and instrumental works.

The great, heroic marker of Ives' compositional life was this working isolation—it is impossible to over-emphasize the strength of effort, commitment, and faith in his own creative vision necessary to fuel the work needed to create his collection of masterpieces, great and small. Supported only (and unfailingly) by his wife Harmony (daughter of the Rev. Joseph Twichell, a close friend of Mark Twain,) and by a handful of sympathetic friends, Ives put pen to paper repeatedly, having no chance to hear his work (except in his inner ear) or gauge its effect in a concert hall filled with listeners, and with no acclaim or support from audiences or colleagues. Ives felt this cultural isolation not only during his mature creative life, but even from his earliest years. America has always, to a greater or lesser extent, found itself distanced from European arts and culture, not only through physical separation but also by the lack of a kind of historical integration; the understanding, knowledge, and appreciation of classical concert music lies much more easily within the web of daily life for most Europeans even today. In America the fine arts continue to be somewhat suspect; in his *Memos*, Ives reflects on this:

> *As a boy [I was] partly ashamed of it ... when other boys, Monday A.M. on vacation, were out driving grocery carts, or doing chores, or playing ball, I felt all wrong to stay in and play piano. And there may be something in it. Hasn't music always been too much an emasculated art?*

Charles Ives' sporadic and infrequent attempts to show his compositions to professional musicians during his creative life were nearly always rebuffed. The greatest of these attempts, which at last began to trigger wider recognition for the composer, was the self-publication of the *Concord* sonata, accompanied by the *Essays Before a Sonata,* sent out to critics and music libraries throughout the States. *The Essays,* which Ives hoped could be used as a tool to help the curious listener or performer dissect the puzzles of this strange new music, ended up partly as a rumination on the same themes which concern the sonata, expressed by other means. More importantly, it clarifies Ives' musical philosophy in general. In wrestling with the great conflict between program music (the tone poem which tells a story or paints a picture) and absolute music (which refers only to its own form and sounds without external references) Ives finds himself exploring a more fundamental question: why do we make music? What does the creative act itself mean? In asking "Can a tune literally represent a stonewall with vines on it ... ?" Ives asks us to consider how pure sound, which means nothing, can come to mean something. (John Cage was to return to this conflict some 60 years later, welding a radical new synthesis of the two approaches in works such as *Apartment House 1776* and *Etcetera*.) Full of wit, self-contradiction, and visionary vigor, it is, alongside Cage's collection of essays in *Silence,* one of the central classics of twentieth-century musical aesthetics.

Various movements, fragments, transcriptions and spin-offs from *Concord* began to be performed throughout the twenties, including the *Emerson Transcriptions* and *The Celestial Railroad*. Eventually, a copy of *Concord* was seen by the young pianist John Kirkpatrick, who was already beginning to focus on new music, and who gave the first public performance of the entire sonata in 1939. It was this performance, in New York City's Town Hall, that caused Lawrence Gilman, the most widely-respected music critic in America, to write:

> *This sonata ... is wide-ranging and capacious. It has passion, tenderness, humor, simplicity, homeliness. It has imagination and spiritual vastness. It has wisdom and beauty and profundity, and a sense of the encompassing terror and splendor of human life and human destiny—a sense of those mysteries that are both human and divine.*

II

Concord has a rich history. The individual movements evolved from a series of orchestral overtures under the heading "Men of Literature" which Ives had planned (of which only the *Robert Browning Overture* was completed). The *Emerson Overture* was conceived as a piano concerto; Ives describes "the orchestra [was] the world and people hearing, and the piano cadenza was Emerson." "Hawthorne" at one point was imagined as requiring "a piano or a dozen pianos." Three pieces eventually sprang from Ives' conception of "Hawthorne," including *The Celestial Railroad* for piano solo and the second movement of the Fourth Symphony. All three share entire passages; all three reflect differing aspects of Hawthorne's fiction, but never, as Ives says, the writer's "basic theme [that has] something ... to do with the influence of sin upon the conscience ... This fundamental part of Hawthorne is not attempted in our music (the 2nd movement of the series) which is but an "extended fragment" trying to suggest some of his wilder, fantastical adventures into the half-childlike, half-fairylike phantasmal realms." "The Alcotts" and "Thoreau," shorter pieces, had their seeds in music for string quartet, flute, and organ.

Ives' sonata, a piece which contains some of the earliest, most notorious, and most striking passages of sustained dissonance, begins with a perfect consonance—the opening B-natural octave. From this singular sound emerges a quickly expanding wedge, inside of which a web of counterpoint anticipates the entire motivic structure of the opening movement. "Emerson" sustains the most controlled and intricate design of any of the sonata's movements, with all of its motives heard in the course of the first two and a half lines of music. The composer himself writes of the two principal themes—the "human faith melody" (begun, but not yet completed, from the fifth note of the piece) and the famous quote from Beethoven's Fifth Symphony, developed as the accented notes work their way down, landing on the C octave at the work's first barline. Ives describes the intention behind his reference:

> We would place its translation above the relentlessness of fate knocking at the door, above the greater human-message of destiny, and strive to bring it towards the spiritual message of Emerson's revelations—even to the "common heart" of Concord—the Soul of humanity knocking at the door of the Divine mysteries, radiant in the faith that it will be opened—and the human become the Divine!

At this first barline we also hear, in the soprano voice, a five-note "sighing" motive, which reaches its apotheosis at the movement's final climax, a page and a half before the end. Pitted contrapuntally against each other in the third line of "Emerson" are the verse melody fully developed on page 8* and the fughetta theme, featured on page 16, followed by the five-note theme of the central Allegro variation set (page 11).

After this explosive mini-exposition Ives launches into what in classic sonata-allegro form would be a first subject, defiant and rhetorical. "Emerson" proceeds via a kind of motivic (rather than harmonic) modulation, the fabric of the music woven from one set of motives which gradually recede giving way to another set—see how the Beethoven notes become less and less prominent on pages 6 and 7 as the rising third of the melodic "second theme" (fully formed by page 8, originally the concerto's slow movement) begins to slip into the texture. "Emerson" hints at sonata-allegro form with this polarity of themes (rhetorical first theme, paired with a contrasting, more lyrical second theme) followed by what would be heard as a development section. However, this "development" abruptly switches into a self-contained set of variations (which began life as the concerto's scherzo) on a theme heard briefly at the end of the opening mini-exposition, closely related to other lyric motives of the movement, but here fully formed for the first time.

The Beethoven notes begin to return (hinting at a "recapitulation"), threaded into a lyrical passage which then gives way to a fughetta inside of which, buried in the forward momentum, we hear the slow movement theme reassert itself. Strikingly, the slow movement theme only returns with its original context intact "moderately and easily" several pages later—but this time, a half-step higher. By this point we are well into the coda of the movement, defined more clearly in the second edition with the *a tempo* shift at the bottom of page 17 taking on a strong *ff* accent (more on this later).

The 6/4 processional implied by the fughetta comes to the fore here, evolving into one of "Emerson's" most striking features—the descending octave line in the left hand. This passacaglia-like motion (similar to the descending whole-step "cello line" in Ives' second string quartet) has appeared earlier in the movement, but now it weaves the entire coda together, submerging unheard for stretches only to surface again with increasing prominence, finally resolving into Beethoven's descending third and bringing "Emerson" to a close.

In the earliest sketches of "Emerson," long stretches of the music are situated in a 6/4 meter. This remains clear in various stretches (some of which retain the regular bar lines—*i.e.,* the passage beginning with the fughetta, page 16) and becomes more ambiguous elsewhere. This regular rhythmic underlay got pushed against, stretched, and fractured over the course of Ives' continued compositional work, to the point where the composer apparently decided to let ambiguity reign and gave up on reoccurring bar lines and a traditionally notated meter for much of the music, yielding one of the most notable and initially notorious aspects of the printed score—few, or no, bar lines for pages at a time.

Formally, the earliest extended sketches towards "Emerson" hint at what Jan Swafford describes as the work's central, radical nature: "the expression of the program, the leading idea, becomes an endless process of composition. The music is an analogue of Emerson's endless quest." (This open-form quality, spiritually anticipating the work of Cage, Brown, Stockhausen and Boulez in the 1950's, puts the lie to the urge to advocate a hard-and-fast choice between the editions.) Ives leaps, in the early orchestral "Emerson Concerto" sketch, from the first two notes at the top of page 5 all the way to the ninth quarter-note (D natural on top of the chord) of page 20 in the first edition. His subsequent work on the music opens up this initial seed in ways that imply the possibility of infinite continuation. The "final" version, retaining an identical outline in the two editions, references classical sonata-allegro form with enough added dislocations, insertions, parentheses, digressions and tangents to reify an open form work as a completely notated one.

One crucial aspect of "Emerson" in which this open-form quality becomes apparent only later is its anticipation of the sonata's final movement. The bi-tonal arpeggios spinning off the brief *forte* return of the "second theme" and leading into the variations (page 10) are made up from the same striking sonority that begins "Thoreau" (A major and E-flat major, two triads separated by a tritone, the same sound Stravinsky featured in *Petrouchka*). We hear this chord again towards the very end of "Emerson"

*All page references refer to this Dover edition.

(interrupting Ives' only extended Beethoven quote, G-G-G-E-flat answered by F-F-F-D), followed by the concluding bars which extend the harmony and could easily lead directly into the opening of "Thoreau," giving to the acute listener the same sense of larger continuity interrupted by tangents that we find within "Emerson."

If in "Emerson" Ives constructs a firmly-controlled, intricate and yet original formal structure, "Hawthorne" shows both a much more discernable and broader formal outline coupled with a vastly more freewheeling thematic approach. (This seems an appropriate response to Nathaniel Hawthorne's contribution to the Concord literary achievement, Hawthorne being the most self-consciously "artistic" of the group, equally or more attentive to the art construct *per se,* as to its underlying philosophy.) "Hawthorne," as John Kirkpatrick and others have pointed out, creates a large, more or less symmetrical arch, traveling from phantasmagoria, through nocturne and ragtime to the central chorale/march reality check, and then backwards to the final virtuoso outburst. Woven through this arch (along with the Beethoven and "human faith" themes) are stretches of sheer virtuosity, evocative effects (the quiet chords of the chorale emerging from underneath *fff* passages of sustained chromatic density), sounds of bells and waltzes, polyrhythms, and several of Ives most remarkable keyboard inventions. The latter includes the famous use of a wooden board (precisely measured) to sound ethereal *pp* clusters which hover above the alto melody (originally conceived as either resonating harmonics or an off-stage piano) and tone clusters played with the palm (more practical than with the fist). Oddly, in significant stretches of "Hawthorne" when the meter is perfectly clear (the ragtime beginning at the bottom of page 37) Ives again does away with barlines (which are not necessary here, of course—but their lack does add to a certain feeling of ambiguity and integrates the occasional rhythmic dislocation more easily). The few remaining barlines feel more like artifacts from early versions. Kirkpatrick, in his heroic effort to "own" the entire sonata as a performer, added many of his own barlines to his personal copy. With over eighty years of having the sonata find its way into the culture along with all the increasingly complex and rhythmically ambiguous compositions which followed, today's performer no longer needs such signposts.

The formal construction of "The Alcotts" and "Thoreau" are simpler than "Emerson" but equally radical in their way. The first large arch of "The Alcotts" builds to Beethoven's theme in his original key of c minor, returning abruptly to the opening B-flat major before descending to the subdominant (and relative major of c minor) for the "old Scotch air" played by Beth Alcott (before "playing at" the Fifth Symphony). Once again the music builds, this time heading to a triumphant C major, sounding the "human faith melody" culminating in Beethoven's four notes, before descending back again and coming to rest on a plain four-part C major chord.

It is here that we hear *Concord's* greatest and most secret revelation. The simple C major triad is transformed into the luminescent harmony which opens "Thoreau"—the complex, bi-tonal "mist and haze" rising from Walden Pond. With this juxtaposition of the simplest and the most complex we hear the reified kernel of Transcendentalism—the unity of the daily and the visionary, the life of the spirit and the life of the body, "to see" as Blake has it, "a World in a Grain of Sand," or, in Ives' words, "a conviction in the power of the common soul which, when all is said and done, may be as typical as any theme of *Concord* and its transcendentalists." This juxtaposition is no less than the great, central truth of Transcendentalism—the simple, plain, easily overlooked domestic virtues and experiences of daily life as windows into a great spiritual vision.

"Thoreau" is as open-ended as "Emerson," through-composed, full of internal rhymes and incomplete repetitions, in a constant state of development yet looping back with recapitulations that are more extrapolation then repetition. The culmination of this process is the ultimate shattering of the solo sonata frame by the introduction of the flute, both programmatic (Thoreau playing his flute at Walden) and formal (a final and most nearly complete statement of the "human faith melody"). When Arnold Schoenberg does something similar, introducing the human voice into his second string quartet, the text clarifies the implications: "I feel the air of another planet…"

After this, the "old oak tree" continues to hum, the ostinato rolls on unending, the evening's "mist and haze" rise again off the pond, Beethoven's motive rings out a final time, refusing "either to rise or fall but is completed where it stands" (Henry Cowell), and the morning's "shadow-thought" returns, subtly altered, with the melody clarifying A major and the harmony hinting at C, G and D major simultaneously, its second phrase rising to the final C sharp, left unresolved, open-ended, in the second edition. Over forty-five minutes after the great thrusting fanfare which opens the first movement, Ives implies that our journey has only begun.

III

This reprint of the first edition of *Concord* opens a number of questions and possibilities for the performer. Unlike earlier composers such as Schumann for whom there are clear and definitive multiple versions of compositions, here there is no need to make a consistent choice between versions. Due to the music's open-ended quality, each performance of *Concord* must be a personal statement, differing from other performances in details as well as interpretive flow, to a more substantial and literal degree than other classical compositions.

The several volumes of *Concord's* first edition which remained in Ives' possession each hold differing and sometimes contradictory alterations and corrections in the composer's hand. Many of the differences between the first and second edition are fairly minor; frequently involving rearticulated notes rather than ties (or vice versa), or local tempo and dynamic indications. These differences are often on the order of a small change of emphasis, implying that no single performance of *Concord* can encompass all possibilities, and even acknowledging the self-contradictory nature of the music (and of the philosophy and writers which inspired the music). This is a piece that will never be finished, and demands but provisional completion at each performance. What William Masselos said of his stereo recording of Ives' First Sonata holds true here as well: "Each time you hear a recording, you think of all the other ways it could have been done. Nevertheless, here is the way it went one morning."

According to Ives editor James Sinclair, in many instances Ives simplified his textures for the original publication of a piece, only to add the complexity back in later (which means that some of the greater complexity in *Concord* may indeed be the sum of Ives' original mature conception of the writing, with the first edition being in actuality a step backwards). In notes to the second edition, Ives writes "This Second Edition in some passages contains more of this [original orchestral] score than does the First Edition, and also has a few revisions made since the First Edition was printed." That said, the outlines of each movement remain the same between the two editions; a few passages include denser harmony and substantial re-writing in the second edition:

- Handfuls of chords which fill out and extend the "sighing" motive at the first barline of "Emerson" into a ff climactic iteration of the Beethoven rhythm in the bass.
- The extensive work-up leading into the return of the Beethoven motive (top of page 9) after its brief absence during "Emerson's" slow movement theme.
- Some increased contrapuntal density on the fughetta starting on page 16; this has consequences which continue to resonate until nearly the final page with the most substantial rewriting of the movement, most notably on the bottom of page 17, where the second edition adds a strong ff to the chord which interrupts the fughetta (Ives calls it "but one of Emerson's sudden calls for a Transcendental Journey"). In the second edition, this includes the climactic fourteen-note chord, three pages from the end.
- The fantastically dense accumulation of sound just before the central hymn of "Hawthorne," where Ives, in the second edition, allows the music to smash into a head-on collision and dead stop which then suddenly disappears, leaving the chorale to sing quietly underneath as though it had been there all along (the great Ives advocate John Heiss refers to this as Ives "bow-and-arrow" technique).
- The distant bell effect at the end of "Hawthorne" which hint at the Beethoven motif (chords in the second edition fill out the two lines of the first edition).

A few other differences include:
- The second edition adds (or restores) the rough transition between the return of the Beethoven theme on page 9 and the return of the "slow movement" theme.
- Ives re-notated the meter of "Emerson's" central variation for the second edition, changing the left hand eighth notes into sixteenth notes, giving an impression of greater fluidity. (In the third variation both editions have sixteenth notes, the result of which is that the variations have a different set of tempo ratios in the two editions. He also removes the arpeggio signs for the right hand chords, giving the second edition a more bell-like quality.)
- Ives asks for a more furiously headlong rush through the end of "Hawthorne in the second edition, where he leaves out the comment "rather evenly but not heavily, though with insistence on the first beat of each three beat group" (page 46), trusting the performer to find the Irish jig swing underlying much of the coda. Also missing from the second edition is "a little slower" at the bottom of page 50 and "from here on, evenly and slower, about $\flat$. = 72" at the top of page 51). Suggestions added later include "rush it" at the ff square in the middle of page 49 and "faster if possible" for the penultimate line of the movement. The *rall.* immediately before slow bells is reduced to a single note (!) for the second edition.
- In "Thoreau", where the "old Elm Tree may feel like humming a phrase from "Down in the Corn Field" at page 60 and again on the final page, Ives tightens the phrases for the second edition, removing a few repeats from the left hand ostinato (he does much the same thing at the top of page 63, making the rhythm more irregular, more forward-moving).
- The outburst which interrupts the return of the Stephen Foster fragment at the bottom of page 63 is more violent in the second edition, hinting at Thoreau's loneliness at Walden (the pond "faintly echoes" this outburst as well as the poet's flute later).
- The differences between the three possible beginnings of the poet's flute song are subtle but notable. In both of the accommodations for solo piano, Ives shortens the first long phrase which introduces the Beethoven reference—substantially in the first edition, to a much smaller degree in the second (possibly even a mistake?), both

retaining a small rhythmic dislocation which interrupts the regular eighth-note pulse of the version with flute.
- Ives made subtle but striking changes to the ends of both "Emerson" and "Thoreau" for the second edition: In "Emerson's" first version, the final left hand octaves which sound forth Beethoven's notes crescendo as they repeat and descend. The second edition, more enigmatically, fades away to pp, hinting at Emerson's unfinished philosophical quest. "Thoreau" becomes equally unfinished in the second version, in which Ives leaves out the final descending major third—Beethoven's three repeated notes hang, in the treble, stationary, with the tenor leaving incomplete its reference to both "Thoreau's" and Beethoven's openings.

In spite of Ives' famous note to the copyist for his orchestral *Fourth of July* ("Mr. Price: Please don't try to make things nice! All the wrong notes are right") there remains the possibility that, in *Concord*, some of the "wrong" notes are indeed wrong, slips of the pen (either the composer's or the engraver's). Always difficult to say with certainty, of course, but consider:

- The contrapuntal line which weaves through the second line of "Emerson" page 6 (and anticipates the variations' theme) generally begins on A flat; at the one exception Ives' added a flat sign before the A in one of his own copies of the first printing.
- The odd tie which connects the final eighth note at the bottom of page 8 with the same eighth note at the top of page 9 could be written as a simple quarter note; Ives' sketch has a dotted quarter on the left hand's A natural, with the tied A flat connecting to the next page, creating a rhythmic dislocation which makes sense of the tied note.
- On the fourth line of page 18 as the slow movement theme returns, the A natural in the bass from the first edition was changed to G natural in the second; this is most likely an engraving error, as the original ink sketch also has A natural.
- The second $f\!f$ indication on page 26 of "Hawthorne" seems poorly placed in the second edition (the first edition makes this clear); here again (as in the climactic chordal variation at the bottom of page 12) the quarter-note B natural is understood as being played only one quarter-note beat after the preceding half-note chord. (It's entirely possible that this kind of rhythmic overlap occurs in the notation elsewhere, e.g. page 45, line 3.)
- The central hymn of "Hawthorne" has a few subtle changes between the editions. One, puzzling but plausible, is the tenor's change from G sharp to A natural for the fourth chord of the hymn's penultimate measure. A natural, because no key signature (with the next pitch in the voice clearly labeled A sharp), but lacking a natural sign which would point to the "wrong" note more clearly.
- The placement of both the $f\!f$ dynamic marking and what seems to be the hymn's final chord following this is also troubling. An accomplished comedian such as Ives would not likely repeat the same joke (the shocking interruption of the hymn with a dissonant blast) in such close succession, especially following a rhythmic hesitation. More likely, the half-note chord, only mildly dissonant, should fall ppp on the downbeat, overlaid onto the tied chord from the previous measure, with the sixteenth-note runs erupting $f\!f$ immediately after.
- After the climactic falling fourths on page 46 of "Hawthorne" the rhythm of the first four notes quoting "Columbia, the Gem of the Ocean" is distorted in an odd way—with the tenor imitation getting it right. If this is a joke it would be way more subtle than one finds anywhere else in Ives, and John Kirkpatrick claims to have heard Ives himself play this passage with the tune's original rhythm (quarter notes for both G and F, followed by a dotted-eighth/sixteenth for D/B flat), apparently never noticing the printed slip.
- And a famous engraving error in "Thoreau," which was ultimately embraced by the delighted composer, is found at the bottom of page 59, where the fifth left hand chord took on an extra leger line, causing a leap up of a third in the tenor to G–A sharp; Ives retained the higher notes for the second edition and reintroduced the second tenor note, also a third higher at B natural.

IV

Concord, while not exactly a staple of concert life, has nonetheless entered the repertoire of a large number of professional and advanced student pianists. Performances can be repeatedly (if not frequently) found in the concert seasons of most major cities and music festivals. This writer has taught several students at the college and graduate level who have presented the entire work, and a larger number who studied single movements. The technical challenges, reputation, scope, and vividness of the music appeal to any serious pianist. John Kirkpatrick's own recording set a standard for all future recordings and performances. An incomplete list of pianists who have recorded *Concord* includes Gilbert Kalish, Pierre-Laurent Aimard, Marc-André Hamelin, Steven Mayer, Herbert Henck, Donna Coleman, Robert Shannon, Yvar Mikhashoff and Easley Blackwood. The German pianist Aloys Kontarsky, well-known for his work with composer Karlheinz Stockhausen, made one of the earliest recordings for Earle Brown's Time-Mainstream label. Alan Mandel was the first to record the collected piano music of Ives.

The challenges of *Concord* are varied and not always apparent. The technical challenges of the work—large chords, speedy passagework, polyphonic differentiation of lines, vivid dynamic and tonal contrasts—are clear on first examination of the score. The use of American vernacular in the sonata creates difficulties for the interpreter who has not grown up immersed in that sound. The second, third, and fourth lines on page 46 of "Hawthorne" seem to be one of the instances Ives refers to in the *Essays* of "something personal, which tries to be 'national' suddenly at twilight, and universal suddenly at midnight." One particularly problematic aspect of "Thoreau" is the refrain-like phrase which sings "Down in the Corn Field," borrowed from Stephen Foster's song "Massa's in de Cold, Cold Ground." The original song has a troubling and complex context, purporting to be a lament sung by slaves mourning the death of their master, written however by a composer who (likely an abolitionist) was to insist that performances of his songs should impart dignity to their African-American characters. For Ives, this writer believes, the isolated phrase (he refers to it only as "Down in the Corn Field") sings only of mourning and solitude, removed from Foster's original context.

Ives' famous quotations borrow not only from other music but from the sounds of the real world as well—the locomotive starting up after the march on page 37, Thoreau hearing church bells (or is it a train whistle) through the woods on the second line of page 61.

Other demands are more conventionally pianistic; "Emerson," in particular, demands an orchestral sound from the piano. Lou Harrison's words in his preface to Ives' first piano sonata are *a propos*:

> *In the tradition of the "Hammerklavier" and the Liszt b minor, [Ives' first] is probably the penultimate romantic sonata, the same composer's* Concord *probably the last ... it should be performed in the manner fitting, making full use of the weighted, full sound of the large grand piano, rich in tone and warm in resonance. The flowing, sumptuous character of the sonata, its range of contemplative and heroic, as well as fantastic, expressions, indicate the "grand manner."*

On page 42 of "Hawthorne" after the cacophonic climax, the performer must connect the gentle tune to sound through the chords.

The "recitative" on the final page of "Emerson" needs to connect through the fermatas in order to be heard as the "sighing" motive from the previous bars.

There are also certain mechanical problems for the performer:

- The emergence of the pianissimo hymn from underneath the preceding cacophony. The first time, the bass G natural tends to ring out too loudly for the rest of the chord, while the soprano note may fade before the pedal release; this writer leaves the low G out from the fast passage and arpeggiates the quiet chord inaudibly beneath the ringing cluster; in the return a short passage later, the low F sharp octave the hymn can be pressed silently—the low strings resonate with the rest of the sound perfectly.

- The thrice-repeated C sharp at the bottom of page 10, descending to the A natural which begins the variations in "Emerson" and is clearly yet another instance of the Beethoven motive. But here the climactic nature of the first three notes seems their own apotheosis, detached from the fourth, no longer a completion but a new beginning. From the sketches it seems clear that the Beethoven reference is deliberate, but how to make this a functional transition? Perhaps the best solution is to refuse to do so, allowing the disjunction its own rough edge and trusting the listener with its implications.

- Ives' dense harmonic and polyphonic conception requires imaginative use of the hands over the two (and frequently three) staves. Determining where the original conception for two hands is best served verbatim, where one hand is required to help the other, and where Ives' own suggestions for distribution of the hands may be accepted or altered (one edition frequently contradicts the other here) is an ongoing task. Frequently the thumbs are called upon to target the cracks between adjacent white keys.

And then there is the matter of the additional instruments—viola in the first movement, flute in the last. This writer feels that the two measures of viola music toward the end of "Emerson" which appears in the 1947 edition, not in the first edition, should be seen as an artifact of the orchestral "Emerson" overture, played as though it were the viola line in an orchestral performance rather than bringing in a viola player. (The line is too short and too inconsequential to support the disruption that an additional player and instrumental color bring to bear; Ives refers to this as "a fragment from viola part of old score—if played here must be much lighter than other parts.") The appearance of the flute at the end of "Thoreau" is a different story, and clearly preferred, offstage and from a distance if at all possible.

Ultimately it is the demand Ives places on the spiritual imagination and insight of the interpreter that provides the final test. A satisfying performance of *Concord* must integrate the range of human experience in the very way that the Transcendentalists sought in their writings. The "mundane" folksy pleasures of common life and the ecstatic vision of spiritual unity must find common ground and be easily interwoven. The great champion of late twentieth-century piano music David Tudor declared *Concord* too difficult for him to play; given his mastery of works like the Pierre Boulez' second sonata and John Cage's *Music of Changes* it seems clear Tudor was not talking about technical issues; this writer believes Tudor was referring to Ives' spiritual or metaphysical demands. (Tudor famously taught himself to read French while preparing the Boulez sonata, in order to read what Boulez was reading when he composed the work.) The challenge Ives presents to the listener as well as to the performer is to believe in transcendence, a "romantic" notion, while speaking in a modern language. This great difficulty of Ives can be gleaned by contrasting Ives' approach to Emerson and Thoreau with that of another great American composer, John Cage. While preparing the Charles Eliot Norton lectures at Harvard, Cage looked carefully at Emerson's writings as a counterweight to his beloved Thoreau, only to discover that he "couldn't stomach Emerson." The emotionally vivid, uncompromising metaphysics and transcendentally Romantic visions of Emerson lie uneasily alongside the strategies of modernist culture.

V

There is a great Man living in this Country – a composer.
He has solved the problem how to preserve one's self and to learn.
He responds to negligence by contempt.
He is not forced to accept praise or blame.
His name is Ives.
—Arnold Schoenberg

STEPHEN DRURY

RECOMMENDED READING

The definitive biography of Charles Ives:

Charles Ives: A Life with Music—Jan Swafford, W. W. Norton & Company.

Also invaluable are:

Charles E. Ives: Memos—John Kirkpatrick, Ed., W. W. Norton & Company.

All Made of Tunes: Charles Ives and the Uses of Musical Borrowing—J. Peter Burkholder, Yale University Press.

Charles Ives and His Music—Henry and Sidney Cowell, Da Capo Press.

Charles Ives Remembered: An Oral History—Vivian Perlis, University of Illinois Press.

Charles Ives: "My Father's Song": A Psychoanalytic Biography—Stuart Feder, Yale University Press.

ESSAYS BEFORE A SONATA

By Charles Ives

"These prefatory essays were written by the composer for those who can't stand his music—and the music for those who can't stand his essays; to those who can't stand either, the whole is respectfully dedicated."

CONTENTS

Introduction	xiv
I. Prologue	xiv
II. Emerson	xvi
III. Hawthorne	xxv
IV. "The Alcotts"	xxvi
V. Thoreau	xxvii
VI. Epilogue	xxxiii

The following pages were written primarily as a preface or reason for the [writer's] second Pianoforte Sonata—"Concord, Mass., 1845,"—a group of four pieces, called a sonata for want of a more exact name, as the form, perhaps substance, does not justify it. The music and prefaces were intended to be printed together, but as it was found that this would make a cumbersome volume they are separate. The whole is an attempt to present [one person's] impression of the spirit of transcendentalism that is associated in the minds of many with Concord, Mass., of over a half century ago. This is undertaken in impressionistic pictures of Emerson and Thoreau, a sketch of the Alcotts, and a Scherzo supposed to reflect a lighter quality which is often found in the fantastic side of Hawthorne. The first and last movements do not aim to give any programs of the life or of any particular work of either Emerson or Thoreau but rather composite pictures or impressions. They are, however, so general in outline that, from some viewpoints, they may be as far from accepted impressions (from true conceptions, for that matter) as the valuation which they purport to be of the influence of the life, thought, and character of Emerson and Thoreau is inadequate.

I. PROLOGUE

How far is anyone justified, be he an authority or a layman, in expressing or trying to express in terms of music (in sounds, if you like) the value of anything, material, moral, intellectual, or spiritual, which is usually expressed in terms other than music? How far afield can music go and keep honest as well as reasonable or artistic? Is it a matter limited only by the composer's power of expressing what lies in his subjective or objective consciousness? Or is it limited by any limitations of the composer? Can a tune literally represent a stonewall with vines on it or with nothing on it, though it (the tune) be made by a genius whose power of objective contemplation is in the highest state of development? Can it be done by anything short of an act of mesmerism on the part of the composer or an act of kindness on the part of the listener? Does the extreme materializing of music appeal strongly to anyone except to those without a sense of humor—or rather with a sense of humor?—or, except, possibly to those who might excuse it, as Herbert Spencer might by the theory that the sensational element (the sensations we hear so much about in experimental psychology) is the true pleasurable phenomenon in music and that the mind should not be allowed to interfere? Does the success of program music depend more upon the program than upon the music? If it does, what is the use of the music, if it does not, what is the use of the program? Does not its appeal depend to a great extent on the listener's willingness to accept the theory that music is the language of the emotions and only that? Or inversely does not this theory tend to limit music to programs?—a limitation as bad for music itself—for its wholesome progress,—as a diet of program music is bad for the listener's ability to digest anything beyond the sensuous (or physical-emotional). To a great extent this depends on what is meant by emotion or on the assumption that the word as used above refers more to the expression, of, rather than to a meaning in a deeper sense—which may be a feeling influenced by some experience perhaps of a spiritual nature in the expression of which the intellect has some part. "The nearer we get to the mere expression of emotion," says Professor Sturt in his *Philosophy of Art and Personality,* "as in the antics of boys who have been promised a holiday, the further we get away from art."

On the other hand is not all music, program-music,—is not pure music, so called, representative in its essence? Is it not program-music raised to the nth power or rather reduced to the minus nth power? Where is the line to be drawn between the expression of subjective and objective emotion? It is easier to know what each is than when each becomes what it is. The "Separateness of Art" theory—that art is not life but a reflection of it—"that art is not vital to life but that life is vital to it," does not help us. Nor does Thoreau who says not that "life is art," but that "life is an art," which of course is a different thing than the foregoing. Tolstoi is even more helpless to himself and to us. For he eliminates further. From his definition of art we may learn little more than that a kick in the back is a work of art, and Beethoven's 9th Symphony is not. Experiences are passed on from one man to another. Abel knew that. And now we know it. But where is the bridge placed?—at the end of the road or only at the end of our vision? Is it all a bridge?—or is there no bridge because there is no gulf? Suppose that a composer writes a piece of music conscious that he is inspired, say, by witnessing an act of great self-sacrifice—another piece by the contemplation of a certain trait of nobility he perceives in a friend's character—and another by the sight of a mountain lake under moonlight. The first two, from an inspirational standpoint would naturally seem to come under the subjective and the last under the objective, yet the chances are, there is something of the quality of both in all. There may have been in the first instance physical action so intense or so dramatic in character that the remembrance of it aroused a great deal more objective emotion than the composer was conscious of while writing the music. In the third instance, the music may have been influenced strongly though subconsciously by a vague remembrance of certain thoughts and feelings, perhaps of a deep religious or spiritual nature, which suddenly came to him upon realizing the beauty of the scene and which overpowered the first sensuous pleasure—perhaps some such feeling as of the conviction of immortality, that Thoreau experienced and tells about in *Walden*. "I penetrated to those meadows ... when the wild river and the woods were bathed in so pure and bright a light as would have waked the dead *if* they had been slumbering in their graves as some suppose. There needs no stronger proof of immortality." Enthusiasm must permeate it, but what it is that inspires an art-effort is not easily determined much less classified. The word "inspire" is used here in the sense of cause rather than effect. A critic may say that a certain movement is not inspired. But that may be a matter of taste—perhaps the most inspired music sounds the least so—to the critic. A true inspiration may lack a true expression unless it is assumed that if an inspiration is not true enough to produce a true expression—(if there be anyone who can definitely determine what a true expression is)—it is not an inspiration at all.

Again suppose the same composer at another time writes a piece of equal merit to the other three, as estimates go; but holds that he is not conscious of what inspired it—that he had nothing definite in mind—that he was not aware of any mental image or process—that, naturally, the actual work in creating something gave him a satisfying feeling of pleasure perhaps of elation. What will you substitute for the mountain lake, for his friend's character, etc.? Will you substitute anything? If so why? If so what? Or is it enough to let the matter rest on the pleasure mainly physical, of the tones, their color, succession, and relations, formal or informal? Can an inspiration come from a blank mind? Well—he tries to explain and says that he was conscious of some emotional excitement and of a sense of something beautiful, he doesn't know exactly what—a vague feeling of exaltation or perhaps of profound sadness.

What is the source of these instinctive feelings, these vague intuitions and introspective sensations? The more we try to analyze the more vague they become. To pull them apart and classify them as "subjective" or "objective" or as this or as that, means, that they may be well classified and that is about all; it leaves us as far from the origin as ever. What does it all mean? What is behind it all? The "voice of God," says the artist, "the voice of the devil," says the man in the front row. Are we, because we are, human beings, born with the power of innate perception of the beautiful in the abstract so that an inspiration can arise through no external stimuli of sensation or experience,—no association with the outward? Or was there present in the above instance, some kind of subconscious, instantaneous, composite image, of all the mountain lakes this man had ever seen blended as kind of overtones with the various traits of nobility of many of his friends embodied in one personality? Do all inspirational images, states, conditions, or whatever they may be truly called, have for a dominant part, if not for a source, some actual experience in life or of the social relation? To think that they do not—always at least—would be a relief; but as we are trying to consider music made and heard by human beings (and not by birds or angels) it seems difficult to suppose that even subconscious images can be separated from some human experience—there must be something behind subconsciousness to produce consciousness, and so on. But whatever the elements and origin of these so-called images are, that they *do* stir deep emotional feelings and encourage their expression is a part of the unknowable we know. They do often arouse something that has not yet passed the border line between subconsciousness and consciousness—an artistic intuition (well named, but)—object and cause unknown!—here is a program!—conscious or subconscious what does it matter? Why try to trace any stream that flows through the garden of consciousness to its source only to be confronted by another problem of tracing this source to its source? Perhaps Emerson in the *Rhodora* answers by not trying to explain

> *That if eyes were made for seeing*
> *Then beauty is its own excuse for being:*
> *Why thou wert there, O, rival of the rose!*
> *I never thought to ask, I never knew;*
> *But, in my simple ignorance, suppose*
> *The self-same Power that brought me there*
>   *brought you.*

Perhaps Sturt answers by substitution: "We cannot explain the origin of an artistic intuition any more than the origin of any other primary function of our nature. But if as I believe civilization is mainly founded on those kinds of unselfish human interests which we call knowledge and morality it is easily intelligible that we should have a parallel interest which we call art closely akin and lending powerful support to the other two. It is intelligible too that moral goodness, intellectual power, high vitality, and strength should be approved by the intuition." This reduces, or rather brings the problem back to a tangible basis namely:—the translation of an artistic intuition into musical sounds approving and reflecting, or endeavoring to approve and reflect, a "moral goodness," a "high vitality," etc., or any other human attribute mental, moral, or spiritual.

Can music do *more* than this? Can it *do* this? and if so who and what is to determine the degree of its failure or success? The composer, the performer (if there be any), or those who have to listen? One hearing or a century of hearings?—and if it isn't successful or if it doesn't fail what matters it?—the fear of failure need keep no one from the attempt for if the composer is sensitive he need but launch forth a countercharge of "being misunderstood" and hide behind it. A theme that the composer sets up as "moral goodness" may sound like "high vitality," to his friend and but like an outburst of "nervous weakness" or only a "stagnant pool" to those not even his enemies. Expression to a great extent is a matter of terms and terms are anyone's. The meaning of "God" may have a billion interpretations if there be that many souls in the world.

There is a moral in the "Nominalist and Realist" that will prove all sums. It runs something like this:

No matter how sincere and confidential men are in trying to know or assuming that they do know each other's mood and habits of thought, the net result leaves a feeling that all is left unsaid; for the reason of their incapacity to know each other, though they use the same words. They go on from one explanation to another but things seem to stand about as they did in the beginning "because of that vicious assumption." But we would rather believe that music is beyond any analogy to word language and that the time is coming, but not in our lifetime, when it will develop possibilities unconceivable now,—a language, so transcendent, that its heights and depths will be common to all mankind.

II. EMERSON

1

It has seemed to the writer, that Emerson is greater—his identity more complete perhaps—in the realms of revelation—natural disclosure—than in those of poetry, philosophy, or prophecy. Though a great poet and prophet, he is greater, possibly, as an invader of the unknown,—America's deepest explorer of the spiritual immensities,—a seer painting his discoveries in masses and with any color that may lie at hand—cosmic, religious, human, even sensuous; a recorder, freely describing the inevitable struggle in the soul's uprise—perceiving from this inward source alone, that every "ultimate fact is only the first of a new series"; a discoverer, whose heart knows, with Voltaire, "that man seriously reflects when left alone," and would then discover, if he can, that "wondrous chain which links the heavens with earth—the world of beings subject to one law." In his reflections Emerson, unlike Plato, is not afraid to ride Arion's Dolphin, and to go wherever he is carried—to Parnassus or to "Musketaquid."

We see him standing on a summit, at the door of the infinite where many men do not care to climb, peering into the mysteries of life, contemplating the eternities, hurling back whatever he discovers there,—now, thunderbolts for us to grasp, if we can, and translate—now placing quietly, even tenderly, in our hands, things that we may see without effort—if we won't see them, so much the worse for us.

We see him,—a mountain-guide, so intensely on the lookout for the trail of his star, that he has no time to stop and retrace his footprints, which may often seem indistinct to his followers, who find it easier and perhaps safer to keep their eyes on the ground. And there is a chance that this guide could not always retrace his steps if he tried—and why should he!—he is on the road, conscious only that, though his star may not lie within walking distance, he must reach it before his wagon can be hitched to it—a Prometheus illuminating a privilege of the Gods—lighting a fuse that is laid towards men. Emerson reveals the less not by an analysis of itself, but by bringing men towards the greater. He does not try to reveal, personally, but leads, rather, to a field where revelation is a harvest-part, where it is known by the perceptions of the soul towards the absolute law. He leads us towards this law, which is a realization of what experience has suggested and philosophy hoped for. He leads us, conscious that the aspects of truth, as he sees them, may change as often as truth remains constant. Revelation perhaps, is but prophecy intensified—the intensifying of its mason-work as well as its steeple. Simple prophecy, while concerned with the past, reveals but the future, while revelation is concerned with all time. The power in Emerson's prophecy confuses it with—or at least makes it seem to approach—revelation. It is prophecy with no time element. Emerson tells, as few bards could, of what will happen in the past, for his future is eternity and the past is a part of that. And so like all true prophets, he is always modern, and will grow modern with the years—for his substance is not relative but a measure of eternal truths determined rather by a universalist than by a partialist. He measured, as Michel Angelo said true artists should, "with the eye and not the hand." But to attribute modernism to his substance, though not to his expression, is an anachronism—and as futile as calling today's sunset modern.

As revelation and prophecy, in their common acceptance are resolved by man, from the absolute and universal, to the relative and personal, and as Emerson's tendency is fundamentally the opposite, it is easier, safer and so apparently clearer, to think of him as a poet of natural and revealed philosophy. And as such, a prophet—but not one to be confused with those singing soothsayers, whose pockets are filled, as are the pockets of conservative-reaction and radical demagoguery in pulpit, street-corner, bank and columns, with dogmatic fortune-tellings. Emerson, as a prophet in these lower heights, was a conservative, in that he seldom lost his head, and a radical, in that he seldom cared whether he lost it or not. He was a born radical as are all true conservatives. He was too much "absorbed by the absolute," too much of the universal to be either—though he could be both at once. To Cotton Mather, he would have been a demagogue, to a real demagogue he would not be understood, as it was with no self interest that he laid his hand on reality. The nearer any subject or an attribute of it, approaches to the perfect truth at its base, the more does qualification become necessary. Radicalism must always qualify itself. Emerson clarifies as he qualifies, by plunging into, rather than "emerging from Carlyle's soul-confusing labyrinths of speculative radicalism." The radicalism that we hear much about today, is not Emerson's kind—but of thinner fiber—it qualifies itself by going to a "root" and often cutting other roots in the process; it is usually impotent as dynamite in its cause and sometimes as harmful to the wholesome progress of all causes; it is qualified by its failure. But the Radicalism of Emerson plunges to all roots, it becomes greater than itself—greater than all its formal or informal doctrines—too advanced and too conservative for any specific result—too catholic for all the churches—for the nearer it is to truth, the farther it is from a truth, and the more it is qualified by its future possibilities.

Hence comes the difficulty—the futility of attempting to fasten on Emerson any particular doctrine, philosophic, or religious theory. Emerson wrings the neck of any law, that would become exclusive and arrogant, whether a definite one of metaphysics or an indefinite one of mechanics. He hacks his way up and down, as near as he can to the absolute, the oneness of all nature both human and spiritual, and to God's benevolence. To him the ultimate of a conception is its vastness, and it is probably this, rather than the "blind-spots" in his expression that makes us incline to go with him but half-way; and then stand and build dogmas. But if we can not follow all the way—if we do not always clearly perceive the whole picture, we are at least free to imagine it—he makes us feel that we are free to do so; perhaps that is the most he asks. For he is but reaching out through and beyond mankind, trying to see what he can of the infinite and its immensities—throwing back to us whatever he can—but ever conscious that he but occasionally catches a glimpse; conscious that if he would contemplate the greater, he must wrestle with the lesser, even though it dims an outline; that he must struggle if he would hurl back anything—even a broken fragment for men to examine and perchance in it find a germ of some part of truth; conscious at times, of the futility of his effort and its message, conscious of its vagueness, but ever hopeful for it, and confident that its foundation, if not its medium is somewhere near the eventual and "absolute good" the divine truth underlying all life. If Emerson must be dubbed an optimist—then an optimist fighting pessimism, but not wallowing in it; an optimist, who does not study pessimism by learning to enjoy it, whose imagination is greater than his curiosity, who seeing the sign-post to Erebus, is strong enough to go the other way. This strength of optimism, indeed the strength we find always underlying his tolerance, his radicalism, his searches, prophecies, and revelations, is heightened and made efficient by "imagination-penetrative," a thing concerned not with the combining but the apprehending of things. A possession, akin to the power, Ruskin says, all great pictures have, which "depends on the penetration of the imagination into the true nature of the thing represented, and on the scorn of the imagination for all shackles and fetters of mere external fact that stand in the way of its suggestiveness"—a possession which gives the strength of distance to his eyes, and the strength of muscle to his soul. With this he slashes down through the loam—nor would he have us rest there. If we would dig deep enough only to plant a doctrine, from one part of him, he would show us the quick-silver in that furrow. If we would creed his *Compensation,* there is hardly a sentence that could not wreck it, or could not show that the idea is no tenet of a philosophy, but a clear (though perhaps not clearly hurled on the canvas) illustration of universal justice—of God's perfect balances; a story of the analogy or better the identity of polarity and duality in Nature with that in morality. The essay is no more a doctrine than the law of gravitation is. If we would stop and attribute too much to genius, he shows us that "what is best written or done by genius in the world, was no one man's work, but came by wide social labor, when a thousand wrought like one, sharing the same impulse." If we would find in his essay on Montaigne, a biography, we are shown a biography of scepticism—and in reducing this to relation between "sensation and the morals" we are shown a true Montaigne—we know the man better perhaps by this less presentation. If we would stop and trust heavily on the harvest of originality, he shows us that this plant—this part of the garden—is but a relative thing. It is dependent also on the richness that ages have put into the soil. "Every thinker is retrospective."

Thus is Emerson always beating down through the crust towards the first fire of life, of death and of eternity. Read where you will, each sentence seems not to point to the next but to the undercurrent of all. If you would label his a religion of ethics or of morals, he shames you at the outset, "for ethics is but a reflection of a divine personality." All the religions this world has ever known, have been but the aftermath of the ethics of one or another holy person; "as soon as character appears be sure love will"; "the intuition of the moral sentiment is but the insight of the perfection of the laws of the soul"; but these laws cannot be catalogued.

If a versatilist, a modern Goethe, for instance, could put all of Emerson's admonitions into practice, a constant permanence would result,—an eternal short-circuit—a focus of equal X-rays. Even the value or success of but one precept is dependent, like that of a ball-game as much on the batting-eye as on the pitching-arm. The inactivity of permanence is what Emerson will not permit. He will not accept repose against the activity of truth. But this almost constant resolution of every insight towards the absolute may get a little on one's nerves, if one is at all partial-wise to the specific; one begins to ask what is the absolute anyway, and why try to look clear through the eternities and the unknowable even out of the other end. Emerson's fondness for flying to definite heights on indefinite wings, and the tendency to over-resolve, becomes unsatisfying to the impatient, who want results to come as they walk. Probably this is a reason that it is occasionally said that Emerson has no vital message for the rank and file. He has no definite message perhaps for the literal, but messages are all vital, as much, by reason of his indefiniteness, as in spite of it.

There is a suggestion of irony in the thought that the power of his vague but compelling vitality, which ever sweeps us on in spite of ourselves, might not have been his, if it had not been for those definite religious doctrines of the old New England theologians. For almost two centuries, Emerson's mental and spiritual muscles had been in training for him in the moral and intellectual contentions, a part of the religious exercise of his forebears. A kind of higher sensitiveness seems to culminate in him. It gives him a power of searching for a wider freedom of soul than theirs. The religion of Puritanism was based to a great extent, on a search for the unknowable, limited only by the dogma of its theology—a search for a path, so that the soul could better be conducted to the next world, while Emerson's transcendentalism was based on the wider search for the unknowable, unlimited in any way or by anything except the vast bounds of innate goodness, as it might be revealed to him in any phenomena of man, Nature, or God. This distinction, tenuous, in spite of the definite-sounding words, we like to believe has something peculiar to Emerson in it. We like to feel that it superimposes the one that makes all transcendentalism but an intellectual state, based on the theory of innate ideas, the reality of thought and the necessity of its freedom. For the philosophy of the religion, or whatever you will call it, of the Concord Transcendentalists is at least, more than an intellectual state—it has even some of the functions of the Puritan church—it is a spiritual state in which both soul *and* mind can better conduct themselves in this world, and also in the next—when the time comes. The search of the Puritan was rather along the path of logic, spiritualized, and the transcendentalist of reason, spiritualized—a difference in a broad sense between objective and subjective contemplation.

The dislike of inactivity, repose and barter, drives one to the indefinite subjective. Emerson's lack of interest in permanence may cause him to present a subjectivity harsher on the outside than is essential. His very universalism occasionally seems a limitation. Somewhere here may lie a weakness—real to some, apparent to others—a weakness in so far as his relation becomes less vivid—to the many; insofar as he over-disregards the personal unit in the universal. If Genius is the most indebted, how much does it owe to those who would, but do not easily ride with it? If there is a weakness here is it the fault of substance or only of manner? If of the former, there is organic error somewhere, and Emerson will become less and less valuable to man. But this seems impossible, at least to us. Without considering his manner or expression here (it forms the general subject of the second section of this paper), let us ask if Emerson's substance needs an affinity, a supplement or even a complement or a gangplank? And if so, of what will it be composed?

Perhaps Emerson could not have risen to his own, if it had not been for his Unitarian training and association with the churchmen emancipators. "Christianity is founded on, and supposes the authority of, reason, and cannot therefore oppose it, without subverting itself." ... "Its office is to discern universal truths, great and eternal principles ... the highest power of the soul." Thus preached Channing. Who knows but this pulpit aroused the younger Emerson to the possibilities of intuitive reasoning in spiritual realms? The influence of men like Channing in his fight for the dignity of human nature, against the arbitrary revelations that Calvinism had strapped on the church, and for the belief in the divine in human reason, doubtless encouraged Emerson in his unshackled search for the infinite, and gave him premises which he later took for granted instead of carrying them around with him. An overinterest, not an underinterest in Christian ideal aims, may have caused him to feel that the definite paths were well established and doing their share, and that for some to reach the same infinite ends, more paths might be opened—paths which would in themselves, and in a more transcendent way, partake of the spiritual nature of the land in quest,—another expression of God's Kingdom in Man. Would you have the indefinite paths *always* supplemented by the shadow of the definite one of a first influence?

A characteristic of rebellion, is that its results are often deepest, when the rebel breaks not from the worst to the greatest, but from the great to the greater. The youth of the rebel increases this characteristic. The innate rebellious spirit in young men is active and buoyant. They could rebel against and improve the millennium. This excess of enthusiasm at the inception of a movement, causes loss of perspective; a natural tendency to undervalue the great in that which is being taken as a base of departure. A "youthful sedition" of Emerson was his withdrawal from the communion, perhaps, the most socialistic doctrine (or rather symbol) of the church—a "commune" above property or class.

Picking up an essay on religion of a rather remarkable-minded boy—perhaps with a touch of genius—written when he was still in college, and so serving as a good illustration in point—we read— "Every thinking man knows that the church is dead." But every thinking man knows that the church-part of the church always has been dead—that part seen by candle-light, not Christ-light. Enthusiasm is restless and hasn't time to see that if the church holds itself as nothing but the symbol of the greater light it is life itself—as a symbol of a symbol it is dead. Many of the sincerest followers of Christ never heard of Him. It is the better influence of an institution that arouses in the deep and earnest souls a feeling of rebellion to make its aims more certain. It is their very sincerity that causes these seekers for a freer vision to strike down for more fundamental, universal, and perfect truths, but with such feverish enthusiasm, that they appear to overthink themselves—a subconscious way of going Godward perhaps. The rebel of the twentieth century says: "Let us discard God, immortality, miracle—but be not untrue to ourselves." Here he, no doubt, in a sincere and exalted moment, confuses

God with a name. He apparently feels that there is a separatable difference between natural and revealed religion. He mistakes the powers behind them, to be fundamentally separate. In the excessive keenness of his search, he forgets that "being true to ourselves" *is* God, that the faintest thought of immortality *is* God, and that God is "miracle." Over-enthusiasm keeps one from letting a common experience of a day translate what is stirring the soul. The same inspiring force that arouses the young rebel, brings later in life a kind of "experience-afterglow," a realization that the soul cannot discard or limit anything. Would you have the youthful enthusiasm of rebellion, which Emerson carried beyond his youth *always* supplemented by the shadow of experience?

Perhaps it is not the narrow minded alone that have no interest in anything, but in its relation to their personality. Is the Christian Religion, to which Emerson owes embryo-ideals, anything but the revelation of God in a personality—a revelation so that the narrow mind could become opened? But the tendency to over-personalize personality may also have suggested to Emerson the necessity for more universal, and impersonal paths, though they be indefinite of outline and vague of ascent. Could you journey, with equal benefit, if they were less so? Would you have the universal always supplemented by the shadow of the personal? If this view is accepted, and we doubt that it can be by the majority, Emerson's substance could well bear a supplement, perhaps an affinity. Something that will support that which some conceive he does not offer. Something that will help answer Alton Locke's question: "What has Emerson for the working-man?" and questions of others who look for the gangplank before the ship comes in sight. Something that will supply the definite banister to the infinite, which it is said he keeps invisible. Something that will point a crossroad from "his personal" to "his nature." Something that may be in Thoreau or Wordsworth, or in another poet whose songs "breathe of a new morning of a higher life though a definite beauty in Nature"—or something that will show the birth of his ideal and hold out a background of revealed religion, as a perspective to his transcendent religion—a counterpoise in his rebellion— which we feel Channing or Dr. Bushnell, or other saints known and unknown might supply.

If the arc must be completed—if there are those who would have the great, dim outlines of Emerson fulfilled, it is fortunate that there are Bushnells, and Wordsworths, to whom they may appeal—to say nothing of the Vedas, the Bible, or their own souls. But such possibilities and conceptions, the deeper they are received, the more they seem to reduce their need. Emerson's Circle may be a better whole, without its complement. Perhaps his "unsatiable demand for unity, the need to recognize one nature in all variety of objects," would have been impaired, if something should make it simpler for men to find the identity they at first want in his substance. "Draw if thou canst the mystic line severing rightly his from thine, which is human, which divine." Whatever means one would use to personalize Emerson's natural revelation, whether by a vision or a board walk, the vastness of his aims and the dignity of his tolerance would doubtless cause him to accept or at least try to accept, and use "magically as a part of his fortune." He would modestly say, perhaps, "that the world is enlarged for him, not by finding new objects, but by more affinities, and potencies than those he already has." But, indeed, is not enough manifestation already there? Is not the asking that it be made more manifest forgetting that "we are not strong by our power to penetrate, but by our relatedness?" Will more signs create a greater sympathy? Is not our weak suggestion needed only for those content with their own hopelessness?

Others may lead others to him, but he finds his problem in making "gladness hope and fortitude flow from his page," rather than in arranging that our hearts be there to receive it. The first is his duty—the last ours!

2

A devotion to an end tends to undervalue the means. A power of revelation may make one more concerned about his perceptions of the soul's nature than the way of their disclosure. Emerson is more interested in what he perceives than in his expression of it. He is a creator whose intensity is consumed more with the substance of his creation than with the manner by which he shows it to others. Like Petrarch he seems more a discoverer of Beauty than an imparter of it. But these discoveries, these devotions to aims, these struggles toward the absolute, do not these in themselves, impart something, if not all, of their own unity and coherence—which is not received, as such, at first, nor is foremost in their expression. It must be remembered that "truth" was what Emerson was after—not strength of outline, or even beauty except in so far as they might reveal themselves, naturally, in his explorations towards the infinite. To think hard and deeply and to say what is thought, regardless of consequences, may produce a first impression, either of great translucence, or of great muddiness, but in the latter there may be hidden possibilities. Some accuse Brahms' orchestration of being muddy. This may be a good name for a first impression of it. But if it should seem less so, he might not be saying what he thought. The mud may be a form of sincerity which demands that the heart be translated, rather than handed around through the pit. A clearer scoring might have lowered the thought. Carlyle told Emerson that some of his paragraphs didn't cohere. Emerson wrote by sentences or phrases, rather than by logical sequence. His underlying plan of work seems based on the large unity of a series of particular aspects of a subject, rather than on the continuity of its expression. As thoughts surge to his mind, he fills the heavens with them, crowds them in, if necessary, but seldom arranges them, along the ground first. Among classroom excuses for Emerson's imperfect coherence and lack of unity, is one that remembers that his essays were made from lecture notes. His habit, often in lecturing, was to compile his ideas as they came to him on a general subject, in scattered notes, and when on the platform, to trust to the mood of the occasion, to assemble them. This seems a specious explanation, though true to fact. Vagueness, is at times, an indication of nearness to a perfect truth. The definite glory of Bernard of Cluny's Celestial City, is more beautiful than true—probably. Orderly reason does not always have to be a visible part of all great things. Logic may possibly require that unity means something ascending in self-evident relation to the parts and to the whole, with no ellipsis in the ascent. But reason may permit, even demand an ellipsis, and genius may not need the self-evident part. In fact, these parts may be the "blind-spots" in the progress of unity. They may be filled with little but repetition. "Nature loves analogy and hates repetition." Botany reveals evolution not permanence. An apparent confusion if lived with long enough may become orderly. Emerson was not writing for lazy minds, though one of the keenest of his academic friends said that, he (Emerson) could not explain many of his own pages. But why should he!—he explained them when he discovered them—the moment before he spoke or wrote them. A rare experience of a moment at daybreak, when something in nature seems to reveal all consciousness, cannot be explained at noon. Yet it is a part of the day's unity. At evening, nature is absorbed by another experience. She dislikes to explain as much as to repeat. It is conceivable, that what is unified form to the author, or composer, may of necessity be formless to his audience. A home-run will cause more unity in the grand stand than in the season's batting average. If a composer once starts to compromise, his work will begin to drag on *him*. Before the end is reached, his inspiration has all gone up in sounds pleasing to his audience, ugly to him—sacrificed for the first acoustic—an opaque clarity, a picture painted for its hanging. Easy unity, like easy virtue, is easier to describe, when judged from its lapses than from its constancy. When the infidel admits God is great, he means only: "I am lazy—it is easier to talk than live." Ruskin also says: "Suppose I like the finite curves best, who shall say I'm right or wrong? No one. It is simply a question of experience." You may not be able to experience a symphony, even after twenty performances. Initial coherence today may be dullness tomorrow probably because formal or outward unity depends so much on repetition, sequences, antitheses, paragraphs with inductions and summaries. Macaulay had that kind of unity. Can you read him today? Emerson rather goes out and shouts: "I'm thinking of the sun's glory today and I'll let his light shine through me. I'll say any damn thing that this inspires me with." Perhaps there are flashes of light, still in cipher, kept there by unity, the code of which the world has not yet discovered. The unity of one sentence inspires the unity of the whole—though its physique is as ragged as the *Dolomites.*

Intense lights—vague shadows—great pillars in a horizon are difficult things to nail signboards to. Emerson's outward-inward qualities make him hard to classify, but easy for some. There are many who like to say that he—even all the Concord men—are intellectuals. Perhaps—but intellectuals who wear their brains nearer the heart than some of their critics. It is as dangerous to determine a characteristic by manner as by mood. Emerson is a pure intellectual to those who prefer to take him as literally as they can. There are reformers, and in "the form" lies their interest, who prefer to stand on the plain, and then insist they see from the summit. Indolent legs supply the strength of eye for their inspiration. The intellect is never a whole. It is where the soul finds things. It is often the only track to the over-values. It appears a whole—but never becomes one even in the stock exchange, or the convent, or the laboratory. In the cleverest criminal, it is but a way to a low ideal. It can never discard the other part of its duality—the soul or the void where the soul ought to be. So why classify a quality always so relative that it is more an agency than substance; a quality that disappears when classified. "The life of the All must stream through us to make the man and the moment great." A sailor with a precious cargo doesn't analyze the water.

Because Emerson had generations of Calvinistic sermons in his blood, some cataloguers, would localize or provincialize him, with the sternness of the old Puritan mind. They make him *that,* hold him *there.* They lean heavily on what they find of the above influence in him. They won't follow the rivers in his thought and the play of his soul. And their cousin cataloguers put him in another pigeon-hole. They label him "ascetic." They translate his outward serenity into an impression of severity. But truth keeps one from being hysterical. Is a demagogue a friend of the people because he will lie to them to make them cry and raise false hopes? A search for perfect truths throws out a beauty more spiritual than sensuous. A sombre dignity of style is often confused by under-imagination and by surface-sentiment, with austerity. If Emerson's manner is not always beautiful in accordance with accepted standards, why not accept a few other standards? He is an ascetic, in that he refuses to compromise content with manner. But a real ascetic is an extremist who has but one height. Thus may come the confusion, of one who says that Emerson carries him high, but then leaves him always at *that* height—no higher—a confusion, mistaking a latent exultation for an ascetic reserve. The rules of Thorough Bass can be applied to his scale of flight no more than they can to the planetary system. Jadassohn, if Emerson were literally a composer, could no more analyze his harmony than a guide-to-Boston could. A microscope might show that he uses chords of the 9th, 11th, or the 99th, but a lens far different tells us they are used with different aims from those of Debussy. Emerson is definite in that his art is based on something stronger than the amusing or at its best the beguiling of a few mortals. If he uses a sensuous chord, it is not for sensual ears. His harmonies may float, if the wind blows in that direction, through a voluptuous atmosphere, but he has not Debussy's fondness for trying to blow a sensuous atmosphere from his own voluptuous cheeks. And so he is an ascetic! There is a distance between jowl and soul—and it is not measured by the fraction of an inch between Concord and Paris. On the other hand, if one thinks that his harmony contains no dramatic chords, because no theatrical sound is heard, let him listen to the finale of "Success," or of "Spiritual Laws," or to some of the poems, "Brahma" or "Sursum Corda," for example. Of a truth his Codas often seem to crystallize in a dramatic, though serene and sustained way, the truths of his subject—they become more active and intense, but quieter and deeper.

Then there comes along another set of cataloguers. They put him down as a "classicist," or a romanticist, or an eclectic. Because a prophet is a child of romanticism—because revelation is classic, because eclecticism quotes from eclectic Hindu Philosophy, a more sympathetic cataloguer may say, that Emerson inspires courage of the quieter kind and delight of the higher kind.

The same well-bound school teacher who told the boys that Thoreau was a naturalist because he didn't like to work, puts down Emerson as a "classic," and Hawthorne as a "romantic." A loud voice made this doubly *true* and *sure* to be on the examination paper. But this teacher of "truth *and* dogma" apparently forgot that there is no such thing as "classicism or romanticism." One has but to go to the various definitions of these to know that. If you go to a classic definition you know what a true classic is, and similarly a "true romantic." But if you go to both, you have an algebraic formula, x = x, a cancellation, an *apercu,* and hence satisfying; if you go to all definitions you have another formula x > x, a destruction, another *apercu,* and hence satisfying. Professor Beers goes to the dictionary (you wouldn't think a college professor would be as reckless as that). And so he can say that "romantic" is "pertaining to the style of the Christian and popular literature of the Middle Ages,"—a Roman Catholic mode of salvation (not this definition but having a definition). And so Prof. B. can say that Walter Scott is a romanticist (and Billy Phelps a classic—sometimes). But for our part Dick Croker is a classic and Job a romanticist. Another professor, Babbitt by name, links up Romanticism with Rousseau, and charges against it many of man's troubles. He somehow likes to mix it up with sin. He throws saucers at it, but in a scholarly, interesting, sincere, and accurate way. He uncovers a deformed foot, gives it a name, from which we are allowed to infer that the covered foot is healthy and named classicism. But no Christian Scientist can prove that Christ never had a stomach ache. *The Architecture of Humanism** tells us that "romanticism consists of ... a poetic sensibility towards the remote, as such." But is Plato a classic or towards the remote? Is Classicism a poor relation of time—not of man? Is a thing classic or romantic because it is or is not passed by that biologic—that indescribable stream-of-change going on in all life? Let us settle the point for "good," and say that a thing is classic if it is thought of in terms of the past and romantic if thought of in terms of the future—and a thing thought of in terms of the present is—well, that is impossible! Hence, we allow ourselves to say, that Emerson is neither a classic or romantic but both—and both not only at different times in one essay, but at the same time in one sentence—in one word. And must we admit it, so is everyone. If you don't believe it, there must be some true definition you haven't seen. Chopin shows a few things that Bach forgot—but he is not eclectic, they say. Brahms shows many things that Bach did remember, so he is an eclectic, they say. Leoncavallo writes pretty verses and Palestrina is a priest, and Confucius inspires Scriabin. A choice is freedom. Natural selection is but one of Nature's tunes. "All melodious poets shall be hoarse as street ballads, when once the penetrating keynote of nature and spirit is sounded—the earth-beat, sea-beat, heart-beat, which make the tune to which the sun rolls, and the globule of blood and the sap of the trees."

An intuitive sense of values, tends to make Emerson use social, political, and even economic phenomena, as means of expression, as the accidental notes in his scale—rather than as ends, even lesser ends. In the realization that they are essential parts of the greater values, he does not confuse them with each other. He remains undisturbed except in rare instances, when the lower parts invade and seek to displace the higher. He was not afraid to say that "there are laws which should not be too well obeyed." To him, slavery was not a social or a political or an economic question, nor even one of morals or of ethics, but one of universal spiritual freedom only. It mattered little what party, or what platform, or what law of commerce governed men. Was man governing himself? Social error and virtue were but relative.

This habit of not being hindered by using, but still going beyond the great truths of living, to the greater truths of life gave force to his influence over the materialists. Thus he seems to us more a regenerator than a reformer—more an interpreter of life's reflexes than of life's facts, perhaps. Here he appears greater than Voltaire or Rousseau and helped, perhaps, by the centrality of his conceptions, he could arouse the deeper spiritual and moral emotions, without causing his listeners to distort their physical ones. To prove that mind is over matter, he doesn't place matter

---
* Geoffrey Scott (Constable & Co.)

over mind. He is not like the man who, because he couldn't afford both, gave up metaphysics for an automobile, and when he ran over a man blamed metaphysics. He would not have us get over-excited about physical disturbance but have it accepted as a part of any progress in culture, moral, spiritual or aesthetic. If a poet retires to the mountain-side, to avoid the vulgar unculture of men, and their physical disturbance, so that he may better catch a nobler theme for his symphony, Emerson tells him that "man's culture can spare nothing, wants all material, converts all impediments into instruments, all enemies into power." The latest product of man's culture—the aeroplane, then sails o'er the mountain and instead of an inspiration—a spray of tobacco-juice falls on the poet. "Calm yourself, Poet!" says Emerson, "culture will convert furies into muses and hells into benefit. This wouldn't have befallen you if it hadn't been for the latest transcendent product of the genius of culture" (we won't say what kind), a consummation of the dreams of poets, from David to Tennyson. Material progress is but a means of expression. Realize that man's coarseness has its future and will also be refined in the gradual uprise. Turning the world upside down may be one of its lesser incidents. It is the cause, seldom the effect that interests Emerson. He can help the cause—the effect must help itself. He might have said to those who talk knowingly about the cause of war—or of the last war, and who would trace it down through long vistas of cosmic, political, moral evolution and what not—he might say that the cause of it was as simple as that of any dog-fight—the "hog-mind" of the minority against the universal mind, the majority. The un-courage of the former fears to believe in the innate goodness of mankind. The cause is always the same, the effect different by chance; it is as easy for a hog, even a stupid one, to step on a box of matches under a tenement with a thousand souls, as under an empty bird-house. The many kindly burn up for the few; for the minority is selfish and the majority generous. The minority has ruled the world for physical reasons. The physical reasons are being removed by this "converting culture." Webster will not much longer have to grope for the mind of his constituency. The majority—the people—will need no intermediary. Governments will pass from the representative to the direct. The hog-mind is the principal thing that is making this transition slow. The biggest prop to the hog-mind is pride—pride in property and the power property gives. Ruskin backs this up—"it is at the bottom of all great mistakes; other passions do occasional good, but whenever pride puts in its word ... it is all over with the artist." The hog-mind and its handmaidens in disorder, superficial brightness, fundamental dullness, then cowardice and suspicion—all a part of the minority (the non-people) the antithesis of everything called soul, spirit, Christianity, truth, freedom—will give way more and more to the great primal truths—that there is more good than evil, that God is on the side of the majority (the people)—that he is not enthusiastic about the minority (the non-people)—that he has made men greater than man, that he has made the universal mind and the over-soul greater and a part of the individual mind and soul—that he has made the Divine a part of all.

Again, if a picture in economics is before him, Emerson plunges down to the things that *are* because they are *better* than they are. If there is a row, which there usually is, between the ebb and flood tide, in the material ocean—for example, between the theory of the present order of competition, and of attractive and associated labor, he would sympathize with Ricardo, perhaps, that labor is the measure of value, but "embrace, as do generous minds, the proposition of labor shared by all." He would go deeper than political economics, strain out the self-factor from both theories, and make the measure of each pretty much the same, so that the natural (the majority) would win, but not to the disadvantage of the minority (the artificial) because this has disappeared—it is of the majority. John Stuart Mill's political economy is losing value because it was written by a mind more "a banker's" than a "poet's." The poet knows that there is no such thing as the perpetual law of supply and demand, perhaps not of demand and supply—or of the wage-fund, or price-level, or increments earned or unearned; and that the existence of personal or public property may not prove the existence of God.

Emerson seems to use the great definite interests of humanity to express the greater, indefinite, spiritual values—to fulfill what he can in his realms of revelation. Thus, it seems that so close a relation exists between his content and expression, his substance and manner, that if he were more definite in the latter he would lose power in the former,—perhaps some of those occasional flashes would have been unexpressed—flashes that have gone down through the world and will flame on through the ages—flashes that approach as near the Divine as Beethoven in his most inspired moments—flashes of transcendent beauty, of such universal import, that they may bring, of a sudden, some intimate personal experience, and produce the same indescribable effect that comes in rare instances, to men, from some common sensation. In the early morning of a Memorial Day, a boy is awakened by martial music—a village band is marching down the street, and as the strains of Reeves' majestic *Seventh Regiment March* come nearer and nearer, he seems of a sudden translated—a moment of vivid power comes, a consciousness of material nobility, an exultant something gleaming with the possibilities of this life, an assurance that nothing is impossible, and that the whole world lies at his feet. But as the band turns the corner, at the soldiers' monument, and the march steps of the Grand Army become fainter and fainter, the boy's vision slowly vanishes—his "world" becomes less and less probable—but the experience ever lies within him in its reality. Later in life, the same boy hears the Sabbath morning bell ringing out from the white steeple at the "Center," and as it draws him to it, through the autumn fields of sumach and asters, a Gospel hymn of simple devotion comes out to him—"There's a wideness in God's mercy"—an instant suggestion of that Memorial Day morning comes—but the moment is of deeper import—there is no personal exultation—no intimate world vision—no magnified personal hope—and in their place a profound sense of a spiritual truth,—a sin within reach of forgiveness—and as the hymn voices die away, there lies at his feet—not the world, but the figure of the Savior—he sees an unfathomable courage, an immortality for the lowest, the vastness in humility, the kindness of the human heart, man's noblest strength, and he knows that God is nothing—nothing but love! Whence cometh the wonder of a moment? From sources we know not. But we do know that from obscurity, and from this higher Orpheus come measures of sphere melodies* flowing in wild, native tones, ravaging the souls of men, flowing now with thousand-fold accompaniments and rich symphonies through all our hearts; modulating and divinely leading them.

3

What is character? In how far does it sustain the soul or the soul it? Is it a part of the soul? And then—what is the soul? Plato knows but cannot tell us. Every new-born man knows, but no one tells us. "Nature will not be disposed of easily. No power of genius has ever yet had the smallest success in explaining existence. The perfect enigma remains." As every blind man sees the sun, so character may be the part of the soul we, the blind, can see, and then have the right to imagine that the soul is each man's share of God, and character the muscle which tries to reveal its mysteries—a kind of its first visible radiance—the right to know that it is the voice which is always calling the pragmatist a fool.

At any rate, it can be said that Emerson's character has much to do with his power upon us. Men who have known nothing of his life, have borne witness to this. It is directly at the root of his substance, and affects his manner only indirectly. It gives the sincerity to the constant spiritual hopefulness we are always conscious of, and which carries with it often, even when the expression is somber, a note of exultation in the victories of "the innate virtues" of man. And it is this, perhaps, that makes us feel his courage—not a self-courage, but a sympathetic one—courageous even to tenderness. It is the open courage of a kind heart, of not forcing opinions—a thing much needed when the cowardly, underhanded courage of the fanatic would *force* opinion. It is the courage of believing in freedom, per se, rather than of trying to force everyone to *see* that you believe in it—the courage of the willingness to be reformed, rather than of reforming—the courage teaching that sacrifice is bravery, and force, fear. The courage of righteous indignation, of stammering eloquence, of spiritual insight, a courage ever contracting or unfolding a philosophy as it grows—a courage that would make the impossible possible. Oliver Wendell Holmes says that Emerson attempted the impossible in the *Over-Soul*—"an overflow of spiritual imagination." But he (Emerson) accomplished the impossible in attempting it, and still leaving it impossible. A courageous struggle to satisfy, as Thoreau says, "Hunger rather than the palate"—the hunger of a lifetime sometimes by one meal. His essay on the Pre-Soul (which he did not write) treats of that part of the over-soul's influence on unborn ages, and attempts the impossible only when it stops attempting it.

Like all courageous souls, the higher Emerson soars, the more lowly he becomes. "Do you think the porter and the cook have no experiences, no wonders for you? Everyone knows as much as the Savant." To some, the way to be humble is to admonish the humble, not learn from them. Carlyle would have Emerson teach by more definite signs, rather than interpret his revelations, or shall we say preach? Admitting all the inspiration and help that *Sartor Resartus* has given in spite of its vaudeville and tragic stages, to many young men getting under way in the life of tailor or king, we believe it can be said (but very broadly said) that Emerson, either in the first or second series of essays, taken as a whole, gives, it seems to us, greater inspiration, partly because his manner is less didactic, less personally suggestive, perhaps less clearly or obviously human than Carlyle's. How direct this inspiration is is a matter of personal viewpoint, temperament, perhaps inheritance. Augustine Birrell says he does not feel it—and he seems not to even indirectly. Apparently "a non-sequacious author" can't inspire him, for Emerson seems to him a "little thin and vague." Is Emerson or the English climate to blame for this? He, Birrell, says a really great author dissipates all fears as to his staying-power. (Though fears for our staying-power, not Emerson's, is what we would like dissipated.) Besides, around a really great author, there are no fears to dissipate. "A wise author never allows his reader's mind to be at large," but Emerson is not a *wise* author. His essay on Prudence has nothing to do with prudence, for to be wise and prudent he must put explanation first, and let his substance dissolve because of it. "How carefully," says Birrell again, "a really great author like Dr. Newman, or M. Renan, explains to you what he is going to do, and how he is going to do it." Personally we like the chance of having a hand in the "explaining." We prefer to look at flowers, but not through a botany, for it seems that if we look at them alone, we see a beauty of Nature's poetry, a direct gift from the Divine, and if we look at botany alone, we see the beauty of Nature's intellect, a direct gift of the Divine—if we look at both together, we see nothing.

---
* Paraphrased from a passage in *Sartor Resartus*.

Thus it seems that Carlyle and Birrell would have it that courage and humility have something to do with "explanation"—and that it is not "a respect for all"—a faith in the power of "innate virtue" to perceive by "relativeness rather than penetration"—that causes Emerson to withhold explanation to a greater degree than many writers. Carlyle asks for more utility, and Birrell for more inspiration. But we like to believe that it is the height of Emerson's character, evidenced especially in his courage and humility that shades its quality, rather than that its virtue is less—that it is his height that will make him more and more valuable and more and more within the reach of all—whether it be by utility, inspiration, or other needs of the human soul.

Cannot some of the most valuable kinds of utility and inspiration come from humility in its highest and purest forms? For is not the truest kind of humility a kind of glorified or transcendent democracy—the practicing it rather than the talking it—the not-wanting to level all finite things, but the being willing to be leveled towards the infinite? Until humility produces that frame of mind and spirit in the artist can his audience gain the greatest kind of utility and inspiration, which might be quite invisible at first? Emerson realizes the value of *"the many,"*—that the law of averages has a divine source. He recognizes the various life-values *in reality*—not by reason of their closeness or remoteness, but because he sympathizes with men who live them, and the *majority* do. "The private store of reason is not great—would that there were a public store for man," cries Pascal, but there is, says Emerson, it is the universal mind, an institution congenital with the common or over-soul. Pascal is discouraged, for he lets himself be influenced by surface political and religious history which shows the struggle of the group, led by an individual, rather than that of the individual led by himself—a struggle as much privately caused as privately led. The main-path of all social progress has been spiritual rather than intellectual in character, but the many bypaths of individual-materialism, though never obliterating the highway, have dimmed its outlines and caused travelers to confuse the colors along the road. A more natural way of freeing the congestion in the benefits of material progress will make it less difficult for the majority to recognize the true relation between the important spiritual and religious values and the less important intellectual and economic values. As the action of the intellect and universal mind becomes more and more identical, the clearer will the relation of all values become. But for physical reasons, the group has had to depend upon the individual as leaders, and the leaders with few exceptions restrained the universal mind—they trusted to the "private store," but now, thanks to the lessons of evolution, which Nature has been teaching men since and before the days of Socrates, the public store of reason is gradually taking the place of the once-needed leader. From the Chaldean tablet to the wireless message this public store has been wonderfully opened. The results of these lessons, the possibilities they are offering for ever coordinating the mind of humanity, the culmination of this age-instruction, are seen today in many ways. Labor Federation, Suffrage Extension, are two instances that come to mind among the many. In these manifestations, by reason of tradition, or the bad-habit part of tradition, the hog-mind of the few (the minority), comes in play. The possessors of this are called leaders, but even these "thick-skins" are beginning to see that the *movement* is the leader, and that they are only clerks. Broadly speaking, the effects evidenced in the political side of history have so much of the physical because the causes have been so much of the physical. As a result the leaders for the most part have been under-average men, with skins thick, wits slick, and hands quick with under-values, otherwise they would not have become leaders. But the day of leaders, as such, is gradually closing—the people are beginning to lead themselves—the public store of reason is slowly being opened—the common universal mind and the common over-soul is slowly but inevitably coming into its own. "Let a man believe in God, not in names and places and persons. Let the great soul incarnated in some poor ... sad and simple Joan, go out to service and sweep chimneys and scrub floors ... its effulgent day beams cannot be muffled..." and then "to sweep and scrub will instantly appear supreme and beautiful actions ... and *all* people will get brooms and mops." Perhaps, if all of Emerson—his works and his life—were to be swept away, and nothing of him but the record of the following incident remained to men—the influence of his soul would still be great. A working woman after coming from one of his lectures said: "I love to go to hear Emerson, not because I understand him, but because he looks as though he thought everybody was as good as he was." Is it not the courage—the spiritual hopefulness in his humility that makes this story possible and true? Is it not this trait in his character that sets him above all creeds—that gives him inspired belief in the common mind and soul? Is it not this courageous universalism that gives conviction to his prophecy and that makes his symphonies of revelation begin and end with nothing but the strength and beauty of innate goodness in man, in Nature and in God, the greatest and most inspiring theme of Concord Transcendental Philosophy, as we hear it.

And it is from such a world-compelling theme and from such vantage ground, that Emerson rises to almost perfect freedom of action, of thought and of soul, in any direction and to any height. A vantage ground, somewhat vaster than Schelling's conception of transcendental philosophy—"a philosophy of Nature become subjective." In Concord it includes the objective and becomes subjective to nothing but freedom and the absolute law. It is this underlying courage of the purest humility that gives Emerson that outward aspect of serenity which is felt to so great an extent in much of his work, especially in his codas and perorations. And within this poised strength, we are conscious of that "original authentic fire" which Emerson missed in Shelley—we are conscious of something that is not dispassionate, something that is at times almost turbulent—a kind of furious calm lying deeply in the conviction of the eventual triumph of the soul and its union with God!

Let us place the transcendent Emerson where he, himself, places Milton, in Wordsworth's apostrophe: "Pure as the naked heavens, majestic, free, so didst thou travel on life's common way in cheerful Godliness."

The Godliness of spiritual courage and hopefulness—these fathers of faith rise to a glorified peace in the depth of his greater perorations. There is an "oracle" at the beginning of the Fifth Symphony—in those four notes lies one of Beethoven's greatest messages. We would place its translation above the relentlessness of fate knocking at the door, above the greater human-message of destiny, and strive to bring it towards the spiritual message of Emerson's revelations—even to the "common heart" of Concord—the Soul of humanity knocking at the door of the Divine mysteries, radiant in the faith that it *will* be opened—and the human become the Divine!

III. HAWTHORNE

The substance of Hawthorne is so dripping wet with the supernatural, the phantasmal, the mystical—so surcharged with adventures, from the deeper picturesque to the illusive fantastic, one unconsciously finds oneself thinking of him as a poet of greater imaginative impulse than Emerson or Thoreau. He was not a greater poet possibly than they—but a greater artist. Not only the character of his substance, but the care in his manner throws his workmanship, in contrast to theirs, into a kind of bas-relief. Like Poe he quite naturally and unconsciously reaches out over his subject to his reader. His mesmerism seeks to mesmerize us—beyond Zenobia's sister. But he is too great an artist to show his hand "in getting his audience," as Poe and Tschaikowsky occasionally do. His intellectual muscles are too strong to let him become over-influenced, as Ravel and Stravinsky seem to be by the morbidly fascinating—a kind of false beauty obtained by artistic monotony. However, we cannot but feel that he would weave his spell over us—as would the Grimms and Aesop. We feel as much under magic as the "Enchanted Frog." This is part of the artist's business. The effect is a part of his art-effort in its inception. Emerson's substance and even his manner has little to do with a designed effect—his thunderbolts or delicate fragments are flashed out regardless—they may knock us down or just spatter us—it matters little to him—but Hawthorne is more considerate; that is, he is more artistic, as men say.

Hawthorne may be more noticeably indigenous or may have more local color, perhaps more national color than his Concord contemporaries. But the work of anyone who is somewhat more interested in psychology than in transcendental philosophy, will weave itself around individuals and their personalities. If the same anyone happens to live in Salem, his work is likely to be colored by the Salem wharves and Salem witches. If the same anyone happens to live in the "Old Manse" near the Concord Battle Bridge, he is likely "of a rainy day to betake himself to the huge garret," the secrets of which he wonders at, "but is too reverent of their dust and cobwebs to disturb." He is likely to "bow below the shriveled canvas of an old (Puritan) clergyman in wig and gown—the parish priest of a century ago—a friend of Whitefield." He is likely to come under the spell of this reverend Ghost who haunts the "Manse" and as it rains and darkens and the sky glooms through the dusty attic windows, he is likely "to muse deeply and wonderingly upon the humiliating fact that the works of man's intellect decay like those of his hands" ... "that thought grows moldy," and as the garret is in Massachusetts, the "thought" and the "mold" are likely to be quite native. When the same anyone puts his poetry into novels rather than essays, he is likely to have more to say about the life around him—about the inherited mystery of the town—than a poet of philosophy is.

In Hawthorne's usual vicinity, the atmosphere was charged with the somber errors and romance of eighteenth century New England,—ascetic or noble New England as you like. A novel, of necessity, nails an art-effort down to some definite part or parts of the earth's surface—the novelist's wagon can't always be hitched to a star. To say that Hawthorne was more deeply interested than some of the other Concord writers—Emerson, for example—in the idealism peculiar to his native land (in so far as such idealism of a country can be conceived of as separate from the political) would be as unreasoning as to hold that he was more interested in social progress than Thoreau, because he was in the consular service and Thoreau was in no one's service—or that the War Governor of Massachusetts was a greater patriot than Wendell Phillips, who was ashamed of all political parties. Hawthorne's art was true and typically American—as is the art of all men living in America who believe in freedom of thought and who live wholesome lives to prove it, whatever their means of expression.

Any comprehensive conception of Hawthorne, either in words or music, must have for its basic theme something that has to do with the influence of sin upon the conscience—something more than the Puritan conscience, but something which is permeated by it. In this relation he is wont to use what Hazlitt calls the "moral power of imagination." Hawthorne would try to spiritualize a guilty conscience. He would sing of the relentlessness of guilt, the inheritance of guilt, the shadow of guilt darkening innocent posterity. All of its sins and morbid horrors, its specters, its phantasmas, and even its hellish hopelessness play around his pages, and vanishing between the lines are the less guilty Elves of the Concord Elms, which Thoreau and Old Man Alcott may have felt, but knew not as intimately as Hawthorne. There is often a pervading melancholy about Hawthorne, as Faguet says of de Musset "without posture, without noise but penetrating." There is at times the mysticism and serenity of the ocean, which Jules Michelet sees in "its horizon rather than in its waters." There is a sensitiveness to supernatural sound waves. Hawthorne feels the mysteries and tries to paint them rather than explain them—and here, some may say that he is wiser in a more practical way and so more artistic than Emerson. Perhaps so, but no greater in the deeper ranges and profound mysteries of the interrelated worlds of human and spiritual life.

This fundamental part of Hawthorne is not attempted in our music (the 2nd movement of the series) which is but an "extended fragment" trying to suggest some of his wilder, fantastical adventures into the half-childlike, half-fairylike phantasmal realms. It may have something to do with the children's excitement on that "frosty Berkshire morning, and the frost imagery on the enchanted hall window" or something to do with "Feathertop," the "Scarecrow," and his "Looking Glass" and the little demons dancing around his pipe bowl; or something to do with the old hymn tune that haunts the church and sings only to those in the churchyard, to protect them from secular noises, as when the circus parade comes down Main Street; or something to do with the concert at the Stamford camp meeting, or the "Slave's Shuffle"; or something to do with the Concord he-nymph, or the "Seven Vagabonds," or "Circe's Palace," or something else in the wonderbook—not something that happens, but the way something happens; or something to do with the "Celestial Railroad," or "Phoebe's Garden," or something personal, which tries to be "national" suddenly at twilight, and universal suddenly at midnight; or something about the ghost of a man who never lived, or about something that never will happen, or something else that is not.

IV. "THE ALCOTTS"

If the dictagraph had been perfected in Bronson Alcott's time, he might now be a great writer. As it is, he goes down as Concord's greatest talker. "Great expecter," says Thoreau; "great feller," says Sam Staples, "for talkin' big ... but his daughters is the gals though—always *doin'* somethin'." Old Man Alcott, however, was usually "doin' somethin'" within. An internal grandiloquence made him melodious without; an exuberant, irrepressible, visionary absorbed with philosophy *as* such; to him it was a kind of transcendental business, the profits of which supported his inner man rather than his family. Apparently his deep interest in spiritual physics, rather than metaphysics, gave a kind of hypnotic mellifluous effect to his voice when he sang his oracles; a manner something of a cross between an inside pompous self-assertion and an outside serious benevolence. But he was sincere and kindly intentioned in his eagerness to extend what he could of the better influence of the philosophic world as he saw it. In fact, there is a strong didactic streak in both father and daughter. Louisa May seldom misses a chance to bring out the moral of a homely virtue. The power of repetition was to them a natural means of illustration. It is said that the elder Alcott, while teaching school, would frequently whip himself when the scholars misbehaved, to show that the Divine Teacher—God—was pained when his children of the earth were bad. Quite often the boy next to the bad boy was punished, to show how sin involved the guiltless. And Miss Alcott is fond of working her story around, so that she can better rub in a moral precept—and the moral sometimes browbeats the story. But with all the elder Alcott's vehement, impracticable, visionary qualities, there was a sturdiness and a courage—at least, we like to think so. A Yankee boy who would cheerfully travel in those days, when distances were long and unmotored, as far from Connecticut as the Carolinas, earning his way by peddling, laying down his pack to teach school when opportunity offered, must possess a basic sturdiness. This was apparently not very evident when he got to preaching his idealism. An incident in Alcott's life helps confirm a theory—not a popular one—that men accustomed to wander around in the visionary unknown are the quickest and strongest when occasion requires ready action of the lower virtues. It often appears that a contemplative mind is more capable of action than an actively objective one. Dr. Emerson says: "It is good to know that it has been recorded of Alcott, the benign idealist, that when the Rev. Thomas Wentworth Higginson, heading the rush on the U.S. Court House in Boston, to rescue a fugitive slave, looked back for his following at the court-room door, only the apostolic philosopher was there cane in hand." So it seems that his idealism had some substantial virtues, even if he couldn't make a living.

The daughter does not accept the father as a prototype—she seems to have but few of her father's qualities "in female." She supported the family and at the same time enriched the lives of a large part of young America, starting off many little minds with wholesome thoughts and many little hearts with wholesome emotions. She leaves memory-word-pictures of healthy, New England childhood days,—pictures which are turned to with affection by middle-aged children,—pictures, that bear a sentiment, a leaven, that middle-aged America needs nowadays more than we care to admit.

Concord village, itself, reminds one of that common virtue lying at the height and root of all the Concord divinities. As one walks down the broad-arched street, passing the white house of Emerson—ascetic guard of a former prophetic beauty—he comes presently beneath the old elms overspreading the Alcott house. It seems to stand as a kind of homely but beautiful witness of Concord's common virtue—it seems to bear a consciousness that its past is *living,* that the "mosses of the Old Manse" and the hickories of Walden are not far away. Here is the home of the "Marches"—all pervaded with the trials and happiness of the family and telling, in a simple way, the story of "the richness of not having." Within the house, on every side, lie remembrances of what imagination can do for the better amusement of fortunate children who have to do for themselves—much-needed lessons in these days of automatic, ready-made, easy entertainment which deaden rather than stimulate the creative faculty. And there sits the little old spinet-piano Sophia Thoreau gave to the Alcott children, on which Beth played the old Scotch airs, and played at the Fifth Symphony.

There is a commonplace beauty about "Orchard House"—a kind of spiritual sturdiness underlying its quaint picturesqueness—a kind of common triad of the New England homestead, whose overtones tell us that there must have been something aesthetic fibered in the Puritan severity—the self-sacrificing part of the ideal—a value that seems to stir a deeper feeling, a stronger sense of being nearer some perfect truth than a Gothic cathedral or an Etruscan villa. All around you, under the Concord sky, there still floats the influence of that human faith melody, transcendent and sentimental enough for the enthusiast or the cynic respectively, reflecting an innate hope—a common interest in common things and common men—a tune the Concord bards are ever playing, while they pound away at the immensities with a Beethoven-like sublimity, and with, may we say, a vehemence and perseverance—for that part of greatness is not so difficult to emulate.

We dare not attempt to follow the philosophic raptures of Bronson Alcott—unless you will assume that his apotheosis will show how "practical" his vision in this world would be in the next. And so we won't try to reconcile the music sketch of the Alcotts with much besides the memory of that home under the elms—the Scotch songs and the family hymns that were sung at the end of each day—though there may be an attempt to catch something of that common sentiment (which we have tried to suggest above)—a strength of hope that never gives way to despair—a conviction in the power of the common soul which, when all is said and done, may be as typical as any theme of Concord and its transcendentalists.

V. THOREAU

Thoreau was a great musician, not because he played the flute but because he did not have to go to Boston to hear "the Symphony." The rhythm of his prose, were there nothing else, would determine his value as a composer. He was divinely conscious of the enthusiasm of Nature, the emotion of her rhythms and the harmony of her solitude. In this consciousness he sang of the submission to Nature, the religion of contemplation, and the freedom of simplicity—a philosophy distinguishing between the complexity of Nature which teaches freedom, and the complexity of materialism which teaches slavery. In music, in poetry, in all art, the truth as one sees it must be given in terms which bear some proportion to the inspiration. In their greatest moments the inspiration of both Beethoven and Thoreau express profound truths and deep sentiment, but the intimate passion of it, the storm and stress of it, affected Beethoven in such a way that he could not but be ever showing it and Thoreau that he could not easily expose it. They were equally imbued with it, but with different results. A difference in temperament had something to do with this, together with a difference in the quality of expression between the two arts. "Who that has heard a strain of music feared lest he would speak extravagantly forever," says Thoreau. Perhaps music is the art of speaking extravagantly. Herbert Spencer says that some men, as for instance Mozart, are so peculiarly sensitive to emotion ... that music is to them but a continuation not only of the expression but of the actual emotion, though the theory of some more modern thinkers in the philosophy of art doesn't always bear this out. However, there is no doubt that in its nature music is predominantly subjective and tends to subjective expression, and poetry more objective tending to objective expression. Hence the poet when his muse calls for a deeper feeling must invert this order, and he may be reluctant to do so as these depths often call for an intimate expression which the physical looks of the words may repel. They tend to reveal the nakedness of his soul rather than its warmth. It is not a matter of the relative value of the aspiration, or a difference between subconsciousness and consciousness but a difference in the arts themselves; for example, a composer may not shrink from having the public hear his "love letter in tones," while a poet may feel sensitive about having everyone read his "letter in words." When the object of the love is mankind the sensitiveness is changed only in degree.

But the message of Thoreau, though his fervency may be inconstant and his human appeal not always direct, is, both in thought and spirit, as universal as that of any man who ever wrote or sang—as universal as it is nontemporaneous—as universal as it is free from the measure of history, as "solitude is free from the measure of the miles of space that intervene between man and his fellows." In spite of the fact that Henry James (who knows almost everything) says that "Thoreau is more than provincial—that he is parochial," let us repeat that Henry Thoreau, in respect to thought, sentiment, imagination, and soul, in respect to every element except that of place of physical being—a thing that means so much to some—is as universal as any personality in literature. That he said upon being shown a specimen grass from Iceland that the same species could be found in Concord is evidence of his universality, not of his parochialism. He was so universal that he did not need to travel around the world to *prove* it. "I have more of God, they more of the road." "It is not worth while to go around the world to count the cats in Zanzibar." With Marcus Aurelius, if he had seen the present he had seen all, from eternity and all time forever.

Thoreau's susceptibility to natural sounds was probably greater than that of many practical musicians. True, this appeal is mainly through the sensational element which Herbert Spencer thinks the predominant beauty of music. Thoreau seems able to weave from this source some perfect transcendental symphonies. Strains from the Orient get the best of some of the modern French music but not of Thoreau. He seems more interested *in* than influenced *by* Oriental philosophy. He admires its ways of resignation and self-contemplation but he doesn't contemplate himself in the same way. He often quotes from the Eastern scriptures passages which were they his own he would probably omit, *i.e.,* the Vedas say "all intelligences awake with the morning." This seems unworthy of "accompanying the undulations of celestial music" found on this same page, in which an "ode to morning" is sung—" the awakening to newly acquired forces and aspirations from within to a higher life than we fell asleep from ... for *all* memorable events transpire in the morning time and in the morning atmosphere." Thus it is not the whole tone scale of the Orient but the scale of a Walden morning—"music in single strains," as Emerson says, which inspired many of the polyphonies and harmonies that come to us through his poetry. Who can be forever melancholy "with Æolian music like this"?

This is but one of many ways in which Thoreau looked to Nature for his greatest inspirations. In her he found an analogy to the Fundamental of Transcendentalism. The "innate goodness" of Nature is or can be a moral influence; Mother Nature, if man will but let her, will keep him straight—straight spiritually and so morally and even mentally. If he will take her as a companion, and teacher, and *not* as a duty or a creed, she will give him greater thrills and teach him greater truths than man can give or teach—she will reveal mysteries that mankind has long concealed. It was the soul of Nature not natural history that Thoreau was after. A naturalist's mind is one predominantly scientific, more interested in the relation of a flower to other flowers than its relation to any philosophy or anyone's philosophy. A transcendent love of Nature and writing "Rhus glabra" after sumach doesn't necessarily make a naturalist. It would seem that although thorough in observation (not very thorough according to Mr. Burroughs) and with a keen perception of the specific, a naturalist—inherently—was exactly what Thoreau was *not*. He seems rather to let Nature put him under her microscope than to hold her under his. He was too fond of Nature to practice vivisection upon her. He would have found that painful, "for was he not a part with her?" But he had this trait of a naturalist, which is usually foreign to poets, even great ones; he observed acutely even things that did not particularly interest him—a useful natural gift rather than a virtue.

The study of Nature may tend to make one dogmatic, but the love of Nature surely does not. Thoreau no more than Emerson could be said to have compounded doctrines. His thinking was too broad for that. If Thoreau's was a religion of Nature, as some say,—and by that they mean that through Nature's influence man is brought to a deeper contemplation, to a more spiritual self-scrutiny, and thus closer to God,—it had apparently no definite doctrines. Some of his theories regarding natural and social phenomena and his experiments in the art of living are certainly not doctrinal in form, and if they are in substance it didn't disturb Thoreau and it needn't us ... "In proportion as he simplifies his life the laws of the universe will appear less complex and solitude will not be solitude, nor poverty poverty, nor weakness weakness. If you have built castles in the air your work need not be lost; that is where they should be, now put the foundations under them." ... "Then we will love with the license of a higher order of beings." Is that a doctrine? Perhaps. At any rate, between the lines of some such passage as this lie some of the fountain heads that water the spiritual fields of his philosophy and the seeds from which they are sown (if indeed his whole philosophy is but one spiritual garden). His experiments, social and economic, are a part of its cultivation and for the harvest—and its transmutation, he trusts to moments of inspiration—"only what is thought, said, and done at a certain rare coincidence is good."

Thoreau's experiment at Walden was, broadly speaking, one of these moments. It stands out in the casual and popular opinion as a kind of adventure—harmless and amusing to some, significant and important to others; but its significance lies in the fact that in trying to practice an ideal he prepared his mind so that it could better bring others "into the Walden-state-of-mind." He did not ask for a literal approval, or in fact for any approval. "I would not stand between any man and his genius." He would have no one adopt his manner of life, unless in doing so he adopts his own—besides, by that time "I may have found a better one." But if he preached hard he practiced harder what he preached—harder than most men. Throughout Walden a text that he is always pounding out is "Time." Time for inside work out-of-doors; preferably out-of-doors, "though you perhaps may have some pleasant, thrilling, glorious hours, even in a poor house." Wherever the place—time there must be. Time to show the unnecessariness of necessities which clog up time. Time to contemplate the value of man to the universe, of the universe to man, man's excuse for being. Time from the demands of social conventions. Time *from* too much labor for some, which means too much to eat, too much to wear, too much material, too much materialism for others. Time *from* the "hurry and waste of life." Time *from* the "St. Vitus Dance."

But, on the other side of the ledger, time *for* learning that "there is no safety in stupidity alone." Time *for* introspection. Time *for* reality. Time *for* expansion. Time *for* practicing the art, of living the art of living. Thoreau has been criticized for practicing his policy of expansion by living in a vacuum—but he peopled that vacuum with a race of beings and established a social order there, surpassing any of the precepts in social or political history. "...for he put some things behind and passed an invisible boundary; new, universal, and more liberal laws were around and within him, the old laws were expanded and interpreted in a more liberal sense and he lived with the license of a higher order"—a community in which "God was the only President" and "Thoreau not Webster was His Orator." It is hard to believe that Thoreau really refused to believe that there was any other life but his own, though he probably did think that there was not any other life besides his own for him. Living for society may not always be best accomplished by living *with* society. "Is there any virtue in a man's skin that you must touch it?" and the "rubbing of elbows may not bring men's minds closer together"; or if he were talking through a "worst seller" (magazine) that "had to put it over" he might say, "forty thousand souls at a ball game does not, necessarily, make baseball the highest expression of spiritual emotion." Thoreau, however, is no cynic, either in character or thought, though in a side glance at himself, he may have held out to be one; a "cynic in independence," possibly because of his rule laid down that "self-culture admits of no compromise."

It is conceivable that though some of his philosophy and a good deal of his personality, in some of its manifestations, have outward colors that do not seem to harmonize, the true and intimate relations they bear each other are not affected. This peculiarity, frequently seen in his attitude towards social-economic problems, is perhaps more emphasized in some of his personal outbursts. "I love my friends very much, but I find that it is of no use to go to see them. I hate them commonly when I am near." It is easier to see what he means than it is to forgive him for saying it. The cause of this apparent lack of harmony between philosophy and personality, as far as they can be separated, may have been due to his refusal "to keep the very delicate balance" which Mr. Van Doren in his *Critical Study of Thoreau* says "it is necessary for a great and good man to keep between his public and private lives, between his own personality and the whole outside universe of personalities." Somehow one feels that if he had kept this balance he would have lost "hitting power." Again, it seems that something of the above depends upon the degree of greatness or goodness. A very great and especially a very good man has no separate private and public life. His own personality though not identical with outside personalities is so clear or can be so clear to them that it appears identical, and as the world progresses towards its inevitable perfection this appearance becomes more and more a reality. For the same reason that all great men now agree, in principle but not in detail, in so far as words are able to communicate agreement, on the great fundamental truths. Someone says: "Be specific—what great fundamentals?" Freedom over slavery; the natural over the artificial; beauty over ugliness; the spiritual over the material; the goodness of man; the Godness of man; God; with all other kindred truths that have been growing in expression through the ages, eras, and civilizations, innate things which once seemed foreign to the soul of humankind. All great men—there are millions of them now—agree on these. Around the relative and the absolute value of an attribute, or quality, or whatever it may be called, is where the fight is. The relative not *from* the absolute—but *of* it. Geniuses—and there are millions of them—differ as to *what* is beautiful and *what* is ugly, as to *what* is right and *what* is wrong—there are many interpretations of God—but they all agree that beauty is better than ugliness and right is better than wrong, and that there is a God—all are one when they reach the essence. Every analysis of a criticism or quality of Thoreau invariably leads back and stands us against the great problems of life and eternity. It is a fair indication of the greatness of his problems and ideals.

The unsympathetic treatment accorded Thoreau on account of the false colors that his personality apparently gave to some of his important ideas and virtues, might be lessened if it were more constantly remembered that a command of his today is but a mood of yesterday and a contradiction tomorrow. He is too volatile to paint, much less to catalogue. If Thoreau did not over-say he said nothing. He says so himself. "I desire to speak somewhere without the bounds like a man in a waking moment to men in their waking moments ... for I am convinced that I cannot exaggerate enough even to lay a foundation for a true expression." For all that, it is not safe to think that he should *never* be taken literally, as for the instance in the sentence above. His extravagance at times involves him but Thoreau never rejoices in it as Meredith seems to. He struggles against it and seems much ashamed of being involved as the latter seems of not being. He seldom gets into the situation of Meredith—timidly wandering around with no clothes after stepping out of one of his involve-densities. This habit may be a part of the novelists' license, for perhaps their inspiration is less original and less natural than that of the poets, as traits of human weakness are unnatural to or "not an innate part with human nature." Perhaps if they (novelists) had broader sources for their inspiration they would hardly become novelists. For the same reason that Shakespeare might have been greater if he hadn't written plays. Some say that true composer will never write an opera because a truly brave man will not take a drink to keep up his courage; which is not the same thing as saying Shakespeare is not the greatest figure in all literature; in fact, it is an attempt to say that many novels, most operas, all Shakespeares, and all brave men and women (rum or no rum) are among the noblest blessings with which God has endowed mankind—because, not being perfect, they are perfect examples pointing to that perfection which nothing has yet attained.

Thoreau's mysticism at times throws him into elusive moods—but an elusiveness held by a thread to something concrete and specific, for he had too much integrity of mind for any other kind. In these moments it is easier to follow his thought than to follow him. Indeed, if he were always easy to follow, after one had caught up with him, one might find that it was not Thoreau.

It is, however, with no mystic rod that he strikes at institutional life. Here again he felt the influence of the great transcendental doctrine of "innate goodness" in human nature—a reflection of the like in nature; a philosophic part which, by the way, was a more direct inheritance in Thoreau than in his brother transcendentalists. For besides what he received from a native Unitarianism a good part must have descended to him through his Huguenot blood from the "eighteenth-century French philosophy." We trace a reason here for his lack of interest in "the church." For if revealed religion is the path between God and man's spiritual part—a kind of formal causeway—Thoreau's highly developed spiritual life felt, apparently unconsciously, less need of it than most men. But he might have been more charitable towards those who do need it (and most of us do) if he had been more conscious of his freedom. Those who look today for the cause of a seeming deterioration in the influence of the church may find it in a wider development of this feeling of Thoreau's; that the need is less because there is more of the spirit of Christianity in the world today. Another cause for his attitude towards the church as an institution is one always too common among "the narrow minds" to have influenced Thoreau. He could have been more generous. He took the arc for the circle, the exception for the rule, the solitary bad example for the many good ones. His persistent emphasis on the value of "example" may excuse this lower viewpoint. "The silent influence of the example of one sincere life ... has benefited society more than all the projects devised for its salvation." He has little patience for the unpracticing preacher. "In some countries a hunting parson is no uncommon sight. Such a one might make a good shepherd dog but is far from being a good shepherd." It would have been interesting to have seen him handle the speculating parson, who takes a good salary—more per annum than all the disciples had to sustain their bodies during their whole lives—from a metropolitan religious corporation for "speculating" on Sunday about the beauty of poverty, who preaches: "Take no thought (for your life) what ye shall eat or what ye shall drink nor yet what ye shall put on ... lay not up for yourself treasure upon earth ... take up thy cross and follow me"; who on Monday becomes a "speculating" disciple of another god, and by questionable investments, successful enough to get into the "press," seeks to lay up a treasure of a million dollars for his old age, as if a million dollars could keep such a man out of the poor-house. Thoreau might observe that this one good example of Christian degeneracy undoes all the acts of regeneracy of a thousand humble five-hundred-dollar country parsons; that it out-influences the "unconscious influence" of a dozen Dr. Bushnells if there be that many; that the repentance of this man who did not "fall from grace" because he never fell into it—that this unnecessary repentance might save this man's own soul but not necessarily the souls of the million head-line readers; that repentance would put this preacher right with the powers that be in this world—and the next. Thoreau might pass a remark upon this man's intimacy with God "as if he had a monopoly of the subject"—an intimacy that perhaps kept him from asking God exactly what his Son meant by the "camel," the "needle"—to say nothing of the "rich man." Thoreau might have wondered how this man *nailed down* the last plank in *his* bridge to salvation, by rising to sublime heights of patriotism, in *his* war against materialism; but would even Thoreau be so unfeeling as to suggest to this exhorter that *his* salvation might be clinched "if he would sacrifice his income" (not himself) and come—in to a real Salvation Army, or that the final triumph, the supreme happiness in casting aside this mere $10,000 or $20,000 every year must be denied him—for was he not captain of the ship—must he not stick to his passengers (in the first cabin—the very first cabin)—not that the *ship* was sinking but that *he* was ... we will go no further. Even Thoreau would not demand sacrifice for sacrifice sake—no, not even from Nature.

Property from the standpoint of its influence in checking natural self-expansion and from the standpoint of personal and inherent right is another institution that comes in for straight and cross-arm jabs, now to the stomach, now to the head, but seldom sparring for breath. For does he not say that "wherever a man goes, men will pursue him with their dirty institutions"? The influence of property, as he saw it, on morality or immorality and how through this it may or should influence "government" is seen by the following: "I am convinced that if all men were to live as simply as I did, then thieving and robbery would be unknown. These take place only in communities where some have got more than is sufficient while others have not enough—

Nec bella fuerunt,
Faginus astabat dum
Scyphus ante dapes—

You who govern public affairs, what need have you to employ punishments? Have virtue and the people will be virtuous." If Thoreau had made the first sentence read: "If all men were like me and were to live as simply," etc., everyone would agree with him. We may wonder here how he would account for some of the degenerate types we are told about in some of our backwoods and mountain regions. Possibly by assuming that they are an instance of perversion of the species. That the little civilizing their forbears experienced rendered these people more susceptible to the physical than to the spiritual influence of nature; in other words; if they had been purer naturists, as the Aztecs for example, they would have been purer men. Instead of turning to any theory of ours or of Thoreau for the true explanation of this condition—which is a kind of pseudo-naturalism—for its true diagnosis and permanent cure, are we not far more certain to find it in the radiant look of humility, love, and hope in the strong faces of those inspired souls who are devoting their lives with no little sacrifice to these outcasts of civilization and nature. In truth, may not mankind find the solution of its eternal problem—find it after and beyond the last, most perfect system of wealth distribution which science can ever devise—after and beyond the last sublime echo of the greatest socialistic symphonies—after and beyond every transcendent thought and expression in the simple example of these Christ-inspired souls—be they Pagan, Gentile, Jew, or angel.

However, underlying the practical or impractical suggestions implied in the quotation above, which is from the last paragraph of Thoreau's *Village,* is the same transcendental theme of "innate goodness." For this reason there must be no limitation except that which will free mankind from limitation, and from a perversion of this "innate" possession: And "property" may be one of the causes of this perversion—property in the two relations cited above. It is conceivable that Thoreau, to the consternation of the richest members of the Bolsheviki and Bourgeois, would propose a policy of liberation, a policy of a limited personal property right, on the ground that congestion of personal property tends to limit the progress of the soul (as well as the progress of the stomach)—letting the economic noise thereupon take care of itself—for dissonances are becoming beautiful—and do not the same waters that roar in a storm take care of the eventual calm? That this limit of property be determined not by the *voice* of the majority but by the *brain* of the majority under a government limited to no national boundaries. "The government of the world I live in is not framed in after-dinner conversation"—around a table in a capital city, for there is no capital—a government of principles not parties; of a few fundamental truths and not of many political expediencies. A government conducted by virtuous leaders, for it will be led by all, for all are virtuous, as then their "innate virtue" will no more be perverted by unnatural institutions. This will not be a millennium but a practical and possible application of uncommon common sense. For is it not sense, common or otherwise, for Nature to want to hand back the earth to those to whom it belongs—that is, to those who have to live on it? Is it not sense, that the average brains like the average stomachs will act rightly if they have an equal amount of the right kind of food to act upon and universal education is on the way with the right kind of food? Is it not sense then that all grown men and women (for *all* are necessary to work out the divine "law of averages") shall have a *direct* not an *indirect* say about the things that go on in this world?

Some of these attitudes, ungenerous or radical, generous or conservative (as you will), towards institutions dear to many, have no doubt given impressions unfavorable to Thoreau's thought and personality. One hears him called, by some who ought to know what they say and some who ought not, a crabbed, cold-hearted, sour-faced Yankee—a kind of a visionary sore-head—a cross-grained, egotistic recluse,—even non-hearted. But it is easier to make a statement than prove a reputation. Thoreau may be some of these things to those who make no distinction between these qualities and the manner which often comes as a kind of by-product of an intense devotion of a principle or ideal. He was rude and unfriendly at times but shyness probably had something to do with that. In spite of a certain self-possession he was diffident in most company, but, though he may have been subject to those spells when words do not rise and the mind seems wrapped in a kind of dull cloth which everyone dumbly stares at, instead of looking through—he would easily get off a rejoinder upon occasion. When a party of visitors came to Walden and some one asked Thoreau if he found it lonely there, he replied: "Only by your help." A remark characteristic, true, rude, if not witty. The writer remembers hearing a schoolteacher in English literature dismiss Thoreau (and a half hour lesson, in which time all of Walden,—its surface—was sailed over) by saying that this author (he called everyone "author" from Solomon down to Dr. Parkhurst) "was a kind of a crank who styled himself a hermit-naturalist and who idled about the woods because he didn't want to work." Some such stuff is a common conception, though not as common as it used to be. If this teacher had had more brains, it would have been a lie. The word *idled* is the hopeless part of this criticism, or rather of this uncritical remark. To ask this kind of a man, who plays all the "choice gems from celebrated composers" literally, always literally, and always with the loud pedal, who plays all hymns, wrong notes, right notes, games, people, and jokes literally, and with the loud pedal, who will die literally and with the loud pedal—to ask this man to smile even faintly at Thoreau's humor is like casting a pearl before a coal baron. Emerson implies that there is one thing a genius must have to be a *genius* and that is "mother wit." ... "Doctor Johnson, Milton, Chaucer, and Burns had it. Aunt Mary Moody Emerson has it and can write scrap letters. Who has it need never write anything but scraps. Henry Thoreau has it." His humor though a part of this wit is not always as spontaneous, for it is sometimes pun shape (so is

Charles Lamb's)—but it is nevertheless a kind that can serenely transport us and which we can enjoy without disturbing our neighbors. If there are those who think him cold-hearted and with but little human sympathy, let them read his letters to Emerson's little daughter, or hear Dr. Emerson tell about the Thoreau home life and the stories of his boyhood—the ministrations to a runaway slave; or let them ask old Sam Staples, the Concord sheriff about him. That he "was fond of a few intimate friends, but cared not one fig for people in the mass," is a statement made in a school history and which is superficially true. He cared too much for the masses—too much to let his personality be "massed"; too much to be unable to realize the futility of wearing his heart on his sleeve but not of wearing his path to the shore of "Walden" for future masses to walk over and perchance find the way to themselves. Some near-satirists are fond of telling us that Thoreau came so close to Nature that she killed him before he had discovered her whole secret. They remind us that he died with consumption but forget that he lived with consumption. And without using much charity, this can be made to excuse many of his irascible and uncongenial moods. You to whom that gaunt face seems forbidding—look into the eyes! If he seems "dry and priggish" to you, Mr. Stevenson, "with little of that large unconscious geniality of the world's heroes," follow him some spring morning to Baker Farm, as he "rambles through pine groves ... like temples, or like fleets at sea, full-rigged, with wavy boughs and rippling with light so soft and green and shady that the Druids would have forsaken their oaks to worship in them." Follow him to "the cedar wood beyond Flint's Pond, where the trees covered with hoary blue berries, spiring higher and higher, are fit to stand before Valhalla." Follow him, but not too closely, for you may see little, if you do—"as he walks in so pure and bright a light gilding its withered grass and leaves so softly and serenely bright that he thinks he has never bathed in such a golden flood." Follow him as "he saunters towards the holy land till one day the sun shall shine more brightly than ever it has done, perchance shine into your minds and hearts and light up your whole lives with a great awakening, light as warm and serene and golden as on a bankside in autumn." Follow him through the golden flood to the shore of that "holy land," where he lies dying as men say—dying as bravely as he lived. You may be near when his stern old aunt in the duty of her Puritan conscience asks him: "Have you made your peace with God"? and you may see his kindly smile as he replies, "I did not know that we had ever quarreled." Moments like these reflect more nobility and equanimity perhaps than geniality—qualities, however, more serviceable to world's heroes.

The personal trait that one who has affection for Thoreau may find worst is a combative streak, in which he too often takes refuge. "An obstinate elusiveness," almost a "contrary cussedness," as if he would say, which he didn't: "If a truth about something is not as I think it ought to be, I'll make it what I think, and it *will* be the truth—but if you agree with me, then I begin to think it may not be the truth." The causes of these unpleasant colors (rather than characteristics) are too easily attributed to a lack of human sympathy or to the assumption that they are at least symbols of that lack instead of to a super-sensitiveness, magnified at times by ill health and at times by a subconsciousness of the futility of actually living out his ideals in this life. It has been said that his brave hopes were unrealized anywhere in his career—but it is certain that they started to be realized on or about May 6, 1862, and we doubt if 1920 will end their fulfillment or his career. But there were many in Concord who knew that within their village there was a tree of wondrous growth, the shadow of which—alas, too frequently—was the only part they were allowed to touch. Emerson was one of these. He was not only deeply conscious of Thoreau's rare gifts but in the *Woodland Notes* pays a tribute to a side of his friend that many others missed. Emerson knew that Thoreau's sensibilities too often veiled his nobilities, that a self-cultivated stoicism ever fortified with sarcasm, none the less securely because it seemed voluntary, covered a warmth of feeling. "His great heart, him a hermit made." A breadth of heart not easily measured, found only in the highest type of sentimentalists, the type which does not perpetually discriminate in favor of mankind. Emerson has much of this sentiment and touches it when he sings of Nature as "the incarnation of a thought," when he generously visualizes Thoreau, "standing at the Walden shore invoking the vision of a thought as it drifts heavenward into an incarnation of Nature." There is a Godlike patience in Nature,—in her mists, her trees, her mountains—as if she had a more abiding faith and a clearer vision than man of the resurrection and immortality!

There comes to memory an old yellow-papered composition of school-boy days whose peroration closed with "Poor Thoreau; he communed with nature for forty odd years, and then died." "The forty odd years,"—we'll still grant that part, but he is over a hundred now, and maybe, Mr. Lowell, he is more lovable, kindlier, and more radiant with human sympathy today, than, perchance, you were fifty years ago. It may be that he is a far stronger, a far greater, an incalculably greater force in the moral and spiritual fibre of his fellow-countrymen throughout the world today than you dreamed of fifty years ago. You, James Russell Lowells! You, Robert Louis Stevensons! You, Mark Van Dorens! with your literary perception, your power of illumination, your brilliancy of expression, yea, and with your love of sincerity, you know your Thoreau, but not my Thoreau—that reassuring and true friend, who stood by me one "low" day, when the sun had gone down, long, long before sunset. You may know something of the affection that heart yearned for but knew it a duty not to grasp; you may know something of the great human passions which stirred that soul—too deep for animate expression—you may know all of this, all there is to know about Thoreau, but you know him not, unless you love him!

And if there shall be a program for our music let it follow his thought on an autumn day of Indian summer at Walden—a shadow of a thought at first, colored by the mist and haze over the pond:

> *Low anchored cloud,*
> *Fountain head and*
> *Source of rivers...*
> *Dew cloth, dream drapery—*
> *Drifting meadow of the air....*

but this is momentary; the beauty of the day moves him to a certain restlessness—to aspirations more specific—an eagerness for outward action, but through it all he is conscious that it is not in keeping with the mood for this "Day." As the mists rise, there comes a clearer thought more traditional than the first, a meditation more calm. As he stands on the side of the pleasant hill of pines and hickories in front of his cabin, he is still disturbed by a restlessness and goes down the white-pebbled and sandy eastern shore, but it seems not to lead him where the thought suggests—he climbs the path along the "bolder northern" and "western shore, with deep bays indented," and now along the railroad track, "where the Æolian harp plays." But his eagerness throws him into the lithe, springy stride of the specie hunter—the naturalist—he is still aware of a restlessness; with these faster steps his rhythm is of shorter span—it is still not the *tempo* of Nature, it does not bear the mood that the genius of the day calls for, it is too specific, its nature is too external, the introspection too buoyant, and he knows now that he must let Nature flow through him and slowly; he releases his more personal desires to her broader rhythm, conscious that this blends more and more with the harmony of her solitude; it tells him that his search for freedom on that day, at least, lies in his submission to her, for Nature is as relentless as she is benignant. He remains in this mood and while outwardly still, he seems to move with the slow, almost monotonous swaying beat of this autumnal day. He is more contented with a "homely burden" and is more assured of "the broad margin to his life; he sits in his sunny doorway ... rapt in revery ... amidst goldenrod, sand-cherry, and sumach ... in undisturbed solitude." At times the more definite personal strivings for the ideal freedom, the former more active speculations come over him, as if he would trace a certain intensity even in his submission. "He grew in those seasons like corn in the night and they were better than any works of the hands. They were not time subtracted from his life but so much over and above the usual allowance." "He realized what the Orientals meant by contemplation and forsaking of works." "The day advanced as if to light some work of his—it was morning and lo! now it is evening and nothing memorable is accomplished..." "The evening train has gone by," and "all the restless world with it. The fishes in the pond no longer feel its rumbling and he is more alone than ever..." His meditations are interrupted only by the faint sound of the Concord bell—'tis prayer-meeting night in the village—"a melody as it were, imported into the wilderness..." "At a distance over the woods the sound acquires a certain vibratory hum as if the pine needles in the horizon were the strings of a harp which it swept ... A vibration of the universal lyre ... Just as the intervening atmosphere makes a distant ridge of earth interesting to the eyes by the azure tint it imparts." ... Part of the echo may be "the voice of the wood; the same trivial words and notes sung by the wood nymph." It is darker, the poet's flute is heard out over the pond and Walden hears the swan song of that "Day" and faintly echoes... Is it a transcendental tune of Concord? 'Tis an evening when the "whole body is one sense," ... and before ending his day he looks out over the clear, crystalline water of the pond and catches a glimpse of the shadow—thought he saw in the morning's mist and haze—he knows that by his final submission, he possesses the "Freedom of the Night." He goes up the "pleasant hillside of pines, hickories," and moonlight to his cabin, "with a strange liberty in Nature, a part of herself."

VI. EPILOGUE

1

The futility of attempting to trace the source or primal impulse of an art-inspiration may be admitted without granting that human qualities or attributes which go with personality cannot be suggested, and that artistic intuitions which parallel them cannot be reflected in music. Actually accomplishing the latter is a problem, more or less arbitrary to an open mind, more or less impossible to a prejudiced mind.

That which the composer intends to represent as "high vitality" sounds like something quite different to different listeners. That which I like to think suggests Thoreau's submission to nature may, to another, seem something like Hawthorne's "conception of the relentlessness of an evil conscience"—and to the rest of our friends, but a series of unpleasant sounds. How far can the composer be held accountable? Beyond a certain point the responsibility is more or less undeterminable. The outside characteristics—that is, the points furthest away from the mergings—are obvious to mostly anyone. A child knows a "strain of joy," from one of sorrow. Those a little older know the dignified from the frivolous—the Spring Song from the season in which the "melancholy days have come" (though is there not a glorious hope in autumn!). But where is the definite expression of late-spring against early-summer, of happiness against optimism? A painter paints a sunset—can he paint the setting sun?

In some century to come, when the school children will whistle popular tunes in quarter-tones—when the diatonic scale will be as obsolete as the pentatonic is now—perhaps then these borderland experiences may be both easily expressed and readily recognized. But maybe music was not intended to satisfy the curious definiteness of man. Maybe it is better to hope that music may always be a transcendental language in the most extravagant sense. Possibly the power of literally distinguishing these "shades of abstraction"—these attributes paralleled by "artistic intuitions" (call them what you will)—is ever to be denied man for the same reason that the beginning and end of a circle are to be denied.

2

There may be an analogy—and on first sight it seems that there must be—between both the state and power of artistic perceptions and the law of perpetual change, that ever-flowing stream partly biological, partly cosmic, ever going on in ourselves, in nature, in all life. This may account for the difficulty of identifying desired qualities with the perceptions of them in expression. Many things are constantly coming into being, while others are constantly going out—one part of the same thing is coming in while another part is going out of existence. Perhaps this is why the above conformity in art (a conformity which we seem naturally to look for) appears at times so unrealizable, if not impossible. It will be assumed, to make this theory clearer, that the "flow" or "change" does not go on in the art-product itself. As a matter of fact it probably does, to a certain extent—a picture, or a song, may gain or lose in value beyond what the painter or composer knew, by the progress and higher development in all art. Keats may be only partially true when he says that "A work of beauty is a joy forever"—a thing that is beautiful *to me,* is a joy *to me,* as long as it remains beautiful *to me*—and if it remains so as long as I live, it is so forever, that is, forever to ME. If he had put it this way, he would have been tiresome, inartistic, but perhaps truer. So we will assume here that this change only goes on in man and nature; and that this eternal process in mankind is paralleled in some way during each temporary, personal life.

A young man, two generations ago, found an identity with his ideals, in Rossini; when an older man in Wagner. A young man, one generation ago, found his in Wagner, but when older in César Franck or Brahms. Some may say that this change may not be general, universal, or natural, and that it may be due to a certain kind of education, or to a certain inherited or contracted prejudice. We cannot deny or affirm this, absolutely, nor will we try to even qualitatively—except to say that it will be generally admitted that Rossini, today, does not appeal to this generation, as he did to that of our fathers. As far as prejudice or undue influence is concerned, and as an illustration in point, the following may be cited to show that training may have but little effect in this connection, at least not as much as usually supposed—for we believe this experience to be, to a certain extent, normal, or at least, not uncommon. A man remembers, when he was a boy of about fifteen years, hearing his music-teacher (and father) who had just returned from a performance of *Siegfried* say with a look of anxious surprise that "somehow or other he felt ashamed of enjoying the music as he did," for beneath it all he was conscious of an undercurrent of "make-believe"—the bravery was make-believe, the love was make-believe, the passion, the virtue, all make-believe, as was the dragon—P. T. Barnum would have been brave enough to have gone out and captured a live one! But, that same boy at twenty-five was listening to Wagner with enthusiasm, his reality was real enough to inspire a devotion. The "Preis-Lied," for instance, stirred him deeply. But when he became middle-aged—and long before the Hohenzollern hog-marched into Belgium—this music had become cloying, the melodies threadbare—a sense of something commonplace—yes—of make-believe came. These feelings were fought against for association's sake, and because of gratitude for bygone pleasures—but the former beauty and nobility were not there, and in their place stood irritating intervals of descending fourths and fifths. Those once transcendent progressions, luxuriant suggestions of Debussy chords of the 9th, 11th, etc., were becoming slimy. An unearned exultation—a sentimentality deadening something within hides around in the music. Wagner seems less and less to measure up to the substance and reality of Cesar Franck, Brahms, d'Indy, or even Elgar (with all his tiresomeness), the wholesomeness, manliness, humility, and deep spiritual, possibly religious feeling of these men seem missing and not made up for by his (Wagner's) manner and eloquence, even if greater than theirs (which is very doubtful).

From the above we would try to prove that as this stream of change flows towards the eventual ocean of mankind's perfection, the art-works in which we identify our higher ideals come by this process to be identified with the lower ideals of those who embark after us when the stream has grown in depth. If we stop with the above experience, our theory of the effect of man's changing nature, as thus explaining artistic progress, is perhaps sustained. Thus would we show that the perpetual flow of the life stream is affected by and affects each individual riverbed of the universal watersheds. Thus would we prove that the Wagner period was normal, because we intuitively recognized whatever identity we were looking for at a certain period in our life, and the fact that it was so made the Franck period possible and then normal at a later period in our life. Thus would we assume that this is as it should be, and that it is not Wagner's content or substance or his lack of virtue, that something in us has made us flow past him and not he past us. But something blocks our theory! Something makes our hypotheses seem purely speculative if not useless. It is men like Bach and Beethoven.

Is it not a matter nowadays of common impression or general opinion (for the law of averages plays strongly in any theory relating to human attributes) that the world's attitude towards the substance and quality and spirit of these two men, or other men of like character, if there be such, has not been affected by the flowing stream that has changed us? But if by the measure of this public opinion, as well as it can be measured, Bach and Beethoven are being flowed past—not as fast perhaps as Wagner is, but if they are being passed at all from this deeper viewpoint, then this "change" theory holds.

Here we shall have to assume, for we haven't proved it, that artistic intuitions can sense in music a weakening of moral strength and vitality, and that it is sensed in relation to Wagner and not sensed in relation to Bach and Beethoven. If, in this common opinion, there is a particle of change toward the latter's art, our theory stands—mind you, this admits a change in the manner, form, external expression, etc., but not in substance. If there is no change here towards the substance of these two men, our theory not only falls but its failure superimposes or allows us to presume a fundamental duality in music, and in all art for that matter.

Does the progress of intrinsic beauty or truth (we assume there is such a thing) have its exposures as well as its discoveries? Does the non-acceptance of the foregoing theory mean that Wagner's substance and reality are lower and his manner higher; that his beauty was not intrinsic; that he was more interested in the repose of pride than in the truth of humility? It appears that he chose the representative instead of the spirit itself,—that he chose consciously or unconsciously, it matters not,—the lower set of values in this dualism. These are severe accusations to bring—especially when a man is a little down as Wagner is today. But these convictions were present some time before he was banished from the Metropolitan. Wagner seems to take Hugo's place in Faguet's criticism of de Vigny that, "The staging to him (Hugo) was the important thing—not the conception—that in de Vigny, the artist was inferior to the poet"; finally that Hugo and so Wagner have a certain *pauvrete de fond*. Thus would we ungenerously make Wagner prove our sum! But it is a sum that won't prove! The theory at its best does little more than suggest something, which if it is true at all, is a platitude, viz.: that progressive growth in all life makes it more and more possible for men to separate, in an art-work, moral weakness from artistic strength.

3

Human attributes are definite enough when it comes to their description, but the expression of them, or the paralleling of them in an art-process, has to be, as said above, more or less arbitrary, but we believe that their expression can be less vague if the basic distinction of this art-dualism is kept in mind. It is morally certain that the higher part is founded, as Sturt suggests, on something that has to do with those kinds of unselfish human interests which we call knowledge and morality—knowledge, not in the sense of erudition, but as a kind of creation or creative truth. This allows us to assume that the higher and more important value of this dualism is composed of what may be called reality, quality, spirit, or substance against the lower value of form, quantity, or manner. Of these terms "substance" seems to us the most appropriate, cogent, and comprehensive for the higher and "manner" for the undervalue. Substance in a human-art-quality suggests the body of a conviction which has its birth in the spiritual consciousness, whose youth is nourished in the moral consciousness, and whose maturity as a result of all this growth is then represented in a mental image. This is appreciated by the intuition, and somehow translated into expression by "manner"—a process always less important than it seems, or as suggested by the foregoing (in fact we apologize for this attempted definition). So it seems that "substance" is too indefinite to analyze, in more specific terms. It is practically indescribable. Intuitions (artistic or not?) will sense it—process, unknown. Perhaps it is an unexplained consciousness of being nearer God, or being nearer the devil—of approaching truth or approaching unreality—a silent something felt in the truth-of-nature in Turner against the truth-of-art in Botticelli, or in the fine thinking of Ruskin against the fine soundings of Kipling, or in the wide expanse of Titian against the narrow-expanse of Carpaccio, or in some such distinction that Pope sees between what he calls Homer's "invention" and Virgil's "judgment"—apparently an inspired imagination against an artistic care, a sense of the difference, perhaps, between Dr. Bushnell's *Knowing God* and knowing *about* God. A more vivid explanation or illustration may be found in the difference between Emerson and Poe. The former seems to be almost wholly "substance" and the latter "manner." The measure in artistic satisfaction of Poe's manner is equal to the measure of spiritual satisfaction in Emerson's "substance." The total value of each man is high, but Emerson's is higher than Poe's because "substance" is higher than "manner"—because "substance" leans towards optimism, and "manner" pessimism. We do not know that all this is so, but we feel, or rather know by intuition that it is so, in the same way we know intuitively that right is higher than wrong, though we can't always tell why a thing is right or wrong, or what is always the difference or the margin between right and wrong.

Beauty, in its common conception, has nothing to do with it (substance), unless it be granted that its outward aspect, or the expression between sensuous beauty and spiritual beauty can be always and distinctly known, which it cannot, as the art of music is still in its infancy. On reading this over, it seems only decent that some kind of an apology be made for the beginning of the preceding sentence. It cannot justly be said that anything that has to do with art has nothing to do with beauty in any degree,—that is, whether beauty is there or not, it has something to do with it. A casual idea of it, a kind of a first necessary-physical impression, was what we had in mind. Probably nobody knows what actual beauty is—except those serious writers of humorous essays in art magazines, who accurately, but kindly, with club in hand, demonstrate for all time and men that beauty is a quadratic monomial; that it *is* absolute; that it *is* relative; that it *is not* relative, that it *is not*... The word "beauty" is as easy to use as the word "degenerate." Both come in handy when one does or does not agree with you. For our part, something that Roussel-Despierres says comes nearer to what we like to think beauty is ... "an infinite source of good ... the love of the beautiful ... a constant anxiety for moral beauty." Even here we go around in a circle—a thing apparently inevitable, if one tries to reduce art to philosophy. But personally, we prefer to go around in a circle than around in a parallelepipedon, for it seems cleaner and perhaps freer from mathematics—or for the same reason we prefer Whittier to Baudelaire—a poet to a genius, or a healthy to a rotten apple—probably not so much because it is more nutritious, but because we like its taste better; we like the beautiful and don't like the ugly; therefore, what we like is beautiful, and what we don't like is ugly—and hence we are glad the beautiful is not ugly, for if it were we would like something we don't like. So having unsettled what beauty is, let us go on.

At any rate, we are going to be arbitrary enough to claim, with no definite qualification, that substance can be expressed in music, and that it is the only valuable thing in it, and moreover that in two separate pieces of music in which the notes are almost identical, one can be of "substance" with little "manner," and the other can be of "manner" with little "substance." Substance has something to do with character. Manner has nothing to do with it. The "substance" of a tune comes from somewhere near the soul, and the "manner" comes from—God knows where.

4

The lack of interest to preserve, or ability to perceive the fundamental divisions of this duality accounts to a large extent, we believe, for some or many various phenomena (pleasant or unpleasant according to the personal attitude) of modern art, and all art. It is evidenced in many ways—the sculptors' over-insistence on the "mold," the outer rather than the inner subject or content of his statue—over-enthusiasm for local color—over-interest in the multiplicity of techniques, in the idiomatic, in the effect as shown, by the appreciation of an audience rather than in the effect on the ideals of the inner conscience of the artist or the composer. This lack of perceiving is too often shown by an over-interest in the material value of the effect. The pose of self-absorption, which some men, in the advertising business (and incidentally in the recital and composing business) put into their photographs or the portraits of themselves, while all dolled up in their purple-dressing-gowns, in their twofold wealth of golden hair, in their cissy-like postures over the piano keys—this pose of "manner" sometimes sounds out so loud that the more their music is played, the less it is heard. For does not Emerson tell them this when he says "What you are talks so loud, that I cannot hear what you say"? The unescapable impression that one sometimes gets by a glance at these public-inflicted trade-marks, and without having heard or seen any of their music, is that the one great underlying desire of these appearing-artists, is to impress, perhaps startle and shock their audiences and at any cost. This may have some such effect upon some of the lady-part (male or female) of their listeners but possibly the members of the men-part, who as boys liked hockey better than birthday-parties, may feel like shocking a few of these picture-sitters with something stronger than their own forzandos.

The insistence upon manner in its relation to local color is wider than a self-strain for effect. If local color is a natural part, that is, a part of substance, the art-effort cannot help but show its color—and it will be a true color, no matter how colored; if it is a part, even a natural part of "manner," either the color part is bound eventually to drive out the local part or the local drive out all color. Here a process of cancellation or destruction is going on—a kind of "compromise" which destroys by deadlock; a compromise purchasing a selfish pleasure—a decadence in which art becomes first dull, then dark, then dead, though throughout this process it is outwardly very much alive,—especially after it is dead. The same tendency may even be noticed if there is over-insistence upon the national in art. Substance tends to create affection; manner prejudice. The latter tends to efface the distinction between the love of both a country's virtue and vices, and the love of only the virtue. A true love of country is likely to be so big that it will embrace the virtue one sees in other countries and, in the same breath, so to speak. A composer born in America, but who has not been interested in the "cause of the Freedmen," may be so interested in "negro melodies," that he writes a symphony over them. He is conscious (perhaps only subconscious) that he wishes it to be "American music." He tries to forget that the paternal negro came from Africa. Is his music American or African? That is the great question which keeps him awake! But the sadness of it is, that if he had been born in Africa, his music might have been just as American, for there is good authority that an African soul under an X-ray looks identically like an American soul. There is a futility in selecting a certain type to represent a "whole," unless the interest in the spirit of the type coincides with that of the whole. In other words, if this composer isn't as deeply interested in the "cause" as Wendell Phillips was, when he fought his way through that anti-abolitionist crowd at Faneuil Hall, his music is liable to be less American than he wishes. If a middle-aged man, upon picking up the *Scottish Chiefs,* finds that his boyhood enthusiasm for the prowess and noble deeds and character of Sir Wm. Wallace and of Bruce is still present, let him put, or try to put that glory into an overture, let him fill it chuck-full of Scotch tunes, if he will. But after all is said and sung he will find that his music is American to the core (assuming that he is an American and wishes his music to be). It will be as national in character as the heart of that Grand Army Grandfather, who read those *Cragmore Tales* of a summer evening, when that boy had brought the cows home without witching. Perhaps the memories of the old soldier, to which this man still holds tenderly, may be turned into a "strain" or a "sonata," and though the music does not contain, or even suggest any of the old war-songs, it will be as sincerely American as the subject, provided his (the composer's) interest, spirit, and character sympathize with, or intuitively coincide with that of the subject.

Again, if a man finds that the cadences of an Apache war-dance come nearest to his soul, provided he has taken pains to know enough other cadences—for eclecticism is part of his duty—sorting potatoes means a better crop next year—let him assimilate whatever he finds highest of the Indian ideal, so that he can use it with the cadences, fervently, transcendentally, inevitably, furiously, in his symphonies, in his operas, in his whistlings on the way to work, so that he can paint his house with them—make them a part of his prayer-book—this is all possible and necessary, if he is confident that they have a part in his spiritual consciousness. With this assurance his music will have everything it should of sincerity, nobility, strength, and beauty, no matter how it sounds; and if, with this, he is true to none but the highest of American ideals (that is, the ideals only that coincide with his spiritual consciousness) his music will be true to itself and incidentally American, and it will be so even after it is proved that all our Indians came from Asia.

The man "born down to Babbitt's Corners," may find a deep appeal in the simple but acute "Gospel Hymns of the New England camp meetin'," of a generation or so ago. He finds in them—some of them—a vigor, a depth of feeling, a natural-soil rhythm, a sincerity, emphatic but inartistic, which, in spite of a vociferous sentimentality, carries him nearer the "Christ of the people" than does the Te Deum of the greatest cathedral. These tunes have, for him, a truer ring than many of those groove-made, even-measured, monotonous, non-rhythmed, indoor-smelling, priest-taught, academic, English or neo-English hymns (and anthems)—well-written, well-harmonized things, well-voice-led, well-counterpointed, well-corrected, and well O.K.'d, by well corrected Mus. Bac. R.F.O.G.'s—personified sounds, correct and inevitable to sight and hearing—in a word, those proper forms of stained-glass beauty, which our over-drilled mechanisms-boy—choirs are limited to. But, if the Yankee can reflect the fervency with which "his gospels" were sung—the fervency of "Aunt Sarah," who scrubbed her life away, for her brother's ten orphans, the fervency with which this woman, after a fourteen-hour work day on the farm, would hitch up and drive five miles, through the mud and rain to "prayer meetin'"—her one articulate outlet for the fullness of her unselfish soul—if he can reflect the fervency of such a spirit, he may find there a local color that will do all the world good. If his music can but catch that "spirit" by being a part with itself, it will come somewhere near his ideal—and it will be American, too, perhaps nearer so than that of the devotee of Indian or negro melody. In other words, if local color, national color, any color, is a true pigment of the universal color, it is a divine quality, it is a part of substance in art—not of manner.

The preceding illustrations are but attempts to show that whatever excellence an artist sees in life, a community, in a people, or in any valuable object or experience, if sincerely and intuitively reflected in his work, and so he himself, is, in a way, a reflected part of that excellence. Whether he be accepted or rejected, whether his music is always played, or never played—all this has nothing to do with it—it is true or false by his own measure. If we may be permitted to leave out two words, and add a few more, a sentence of Hegel appears to sum up this idea, "The universal need for expression in art lies in man's rational impulse to exalt the inner ... world (*i.e.,* the highest ideals he sees in the inner life of others) together with what he finds in his own life—into a spiritual consciousness for himself." The artist does feel or does not feel that a sympathy has been approved by an artistic intuition and so reflected in his work. Whether he feels this sympathy is true or not in the final analysis, is a thing probably that no one but he (the artist) knows but the truer he feels it, the more substance it has, or as Sturt puts it, "his work *is* art, so long as he feels in doing it as true artists feel, and so long as his object is akin to the objects that true artists admire."

Dr. Griggs in an Essay on Debussy* asks if this composer's content is worthy the manner. Perhaps so, perhaps not—Debussy himself, doubtless, could not give a positive answer. He would better know how true his feeling and sympathy was, and anyone else's personal opinion can be of but little help here.

We might offer the suggestion that Debussy's content would have been worthier his manner, if he had hoed corn or sold newspapers for a living, for in this way he might have gained a deeper vitality and truer theme to sing at night and of a Sunday. Or we might say that what substance there is, is "too coherent"—it is too clearly expressed in the first thirty seconds. There you have the "whole fragment,"

---

* John C. Griggs, "Debussy" Yale Review, 1914.

a translucent syllogism, but then the reality, the spirit, the substance stops and the "form," the "perfume," the "manner," shimmer right along, as the soapsuds glisten after one has finished washing. Or we might say that his substance would have been worthier, if his adoration or contemplation of Nature, which is often a part of it, and which rises to great heights, as is felt for example, in *La Mer,* had been more the quality of Thoreau's. Debussy's attitude toward Nature seems to have a kind of sensual sensuousness underlying it, while Thoreau's is a kind of spiritual sensuousness. It is rare to find a farmer or peasant whose enthusiasm for the beauty in Nature finds outward expression to compare with that of the city-man who comes out for a Sunday in the country, but Thoreau is that rare country-man and Debussy the city-man with his weekend flights into country-aesthetics. We would be inclined to say that Thoreau leaned towards substance and Debussy towards manner.

5

There comes from Concord, an offer to every mind—the choice between repose and truth, and God makes the offer. "Take which you please ... between these, as a pendulum, man oscillates. He in whom the love of repose predominates will accept the first creed, the first philosophy, the first political party he meets," most likely his father's. He gets rest, commodity, and reputation. Here is another aspect of art-duality, but it is more drastic than ours, as it would eliminate one part or the other. A man may aim as high as Beethoven or as high as Richard Strauss. In the former case the shot may go far below the mark; in truth, it has not been reached since that "thunder storm of 1828" and there is little chance that it will be reached by anyone living today, but that matters not, the shot will never rebound and destroy the marksman. But, in the latter case, the shot may often hit the mark, but as often rebound and harden, if not destroy, the shooter's heart—even his soul. What matters it, men say, he will then find rest, commodity, and reputation—what matters it—if he find there but few perfect truths—what matters (men say)—he will find there perfect media, those perfect instruments of getting in the way of perfect truths.

This choice tells why Beethoven is always modern and Strauss always mediaeval—try as he may to cover it up in new bottles. He has chosen to capitalize a "talent"—he has chosen the complexity of media, the shining hardness of externals, repose, against the inner, invisible activity of truth. He has chosen the first creed, the easy creed, the philosophy of his fathers, among whom he found a half-idiot-genius (Nietzsche). His choice naturally leads him to glorify and to magnify all kinds of dull things—stretched-out *geigermusik*—which in turn naturally leads him to "windmills" and "human heads on silver platters." Magnifying the dull into the colossal, produces a kind of "comfort"—the comfort of a woman who takes more pleasure in the fit of fashionable clothes than in a healthy body—the kind of comfort that has brought so many "adventures of baby-carriages at county fairs"—"the sensation of Teddy bears, smoking their first cigarette"—on the program of symphony orchestras of one hundred performers,—the lure of the media—the means—not the end—but the finish,—thus the failure to perceive that thoughts and memories of childhood are too tender, and some of them too sacred to be worn lightly on the sleeve. Life is too short for these one hundred men, to say nothing of the composer and the "dress-circle," to spend an afternoon in this way. They are but like the rest of us, and have only the expectancy of the mortality-table to survive—perhaps only this "piece." We cannot but feel that a too great desire for "repose" accounts for such phenomena. A MS score is brought to a concertmaster—he may be a violinist—he is kindly disposed, he looks it over, and casually fastens on a passage "that's bad for the fiddles, it doesn't hang just right, write it like this, they will play it better." But that one phrase is the germ of the whole thing. "Never mind, it will fit the hand better this way—it will sound better." My God! what has sound got to do with music! The waiter brings the only fresh egg he has, but the man at breakfast sends it back because it doesn't fit his eggcup. Why can't music go out in the same way it comes in to a man, without having to crawl over a fence of sounds, thoraxes, catguts, wire, wood, and brass? Consecutive-fifths are as harmless as blue laws compared with the relentless tyranny of the "media." The instrument!—there is the perennial difficulty—there is music's limitations. Why must the scarecrow of the keyboard—the tyrant in terms of the mechanism (be it Caruso or a Jew's-harp) stare into every measure? Is it the composer's fault that man has only ten fingers? Why can't a musical thought be presented as it is born—perchance "a bastard of the slums," or a "daughter of a bishop"—and if it happens to go better later on a bass-drum (than upon a harp) get a good bass-drummer.* That music must be heard, is not essential—what it *sounds* like may not be what it is. Perhaps the day is coming when music—believers will learn "that silence is a solvent ... that gives us leave to be universal" rather than personal.

Some fiddler was once honest or brave enough, or perhaps ignorant enough, to say that Beethoven didn't know how to write for the violin,—that, maybe, is one of the many reasons Beethoven is not a Vieuxtemps. Another man says Beethoven's piano sonatas are not pianistic—with a little effort, perhaps, Beethoven could have become a Thalberg. His symphonies are perfect-truths and perfect for the orchestra of 1820—but Mahler could have made

---

* The first movement (Emerson) of the music, which is the cause of all these words, was first thought of (we believe) in terms of a large orchestra, the second (Hawthorne) in terms of a piano or a dozen pianos, the third (Alcotts)—of an organ (or piano with voice or violin), and the last (Thoreau), in terms of strings, colored possibly with a flute or horn.

them—possibly did make them—we will say, "more perfect," as far as their media clothes are concerned, and Beethoven is today big enough to rather like it. He is probably in the same amiable state of mind that the Jesuit priest said, "God was in," when He looked down on the camp ground and saw the priest sleeping with a Congregational Chaplain. Or in the same state of mind you'll be in when you look down and see the sexton keeping your tombstone up to date. The truth of Joachim offsets the repose of Paganini and Kubelik. The repose and reputation of a successful pianist—(whatever that means) who plays Chopin so cleverly that he covers up a sensuality, and in such a way that the purest-minded see nothing but sensuous beauty in it, which, by the way, doesn't disturb him as much as the size of his income-tax—the repose and fame of this man is offset by the truth and obscurity of the village organist who plays Lowell Mason and Bach with such affection that he would give his life rather than lose them. The truth and courage of this organist, who risks his job, to fight the prejudice of the congregation, offset the repose and large salary of a more celebrated choirmaster, who holds his job by lowering his ideals, who is willing to let the organ smirk under an insipid, easy-sounding barcarolle for the offertory, who is willing to please the sentimental ears of the music committee (and its wives)—who is more willing to observe these forms of politeness than to stand up for a stronger and deeper music of simple devotion, and for a service of a spiritual unity, the kind of thing that Mr. Bossitt, who owns the biggest country place, the biggest bank, and the biggest "House of God" in town (for is it not the divine handiwork of his *own*—pocketbook)—the kind of music that this man, his wife, and *his* party (of property right in pews) can't stand because it isn't "pretty."

The doctrine of this "choice" may be extended to the distinction between literal-enthusiasm and natural-enthusiasm (right or wrong notes, good or bad tones against good or bad interpretation, good or bad sentiment) or between observation and introspection, or to the distinction between remembering and dreaming. Strauss remembers, Beethoven dreams. We see this distinction also in Goethe's confusion of the moral with the intellectual. There is no such confusion in Beethoven—to him they are one. It is told, and the story is so well known that we hesitate to repeat it here, that both these men were standing in the street one day when the Emperor drove by—Goethe, like the rest of the crowd, bowed and uncovered—but Beethoven stood bolt upright, and refused even to salute, saying: "Let him bow to us, for ours is a nobler empire." Goethe's *mind* knew this was true, but his moral courage was not instinctive.

This remembering faculty of "repose," throws the mind in unguarded moments quite naturally towards "manner" and thus to the many things the media can do. It brings on an itching to over-use them—to be original (if anyone will tell what that is) with nothing but numbers to be original with. We are told that a conductor (of the orchestra) has written a symphony requiring an orchestra of one hundred and fifty men. If his work perhaps had one hundred and fifty valuable ideas, the one hundred and fifty men might be justifiable—but as it probably contains not more than a dozen, the composer may be unconsciously ashamed of them, and glad to cover them up under a hundred and fifty men. A man may become famous because he is able to eat nineteen dinners a day, but posterity will decorate his stomach, not his brain.

Manner breeds a cussed-cleverness—only to be clever—a satellite of super-industrialism, and perhaps to be witty in the bargain, not the wit in mother-wit, but a kind of indoor, artificial, mental arrangement of things quickly put together and which have been learned and studied—it is of the material and stays there, while humor is of the emotional and of the approaching spiritual. Even Dukas, and perhaps other Gauls, in their critical heart of hearts, may admit that "wit" in music, is as impossible as "wit" at a funeral. The wit is evidence of its lack. Mark Twain could be humorous at the death of his dearest friend, but in such a way as to put a blessing into the heart of the bereaved. Humor in music has the same possibilities. But its quantity has a serious effect on its quality, "inverse ratio" is a good formula to adopt here. Comedy has its part, but wit never. Strauss is at his best in these lower rooms, but his comedy reminds us more of the physical fun of Lever rather than "comedy in the Meredithian sense" as Mason suggests. Meredith is a little too deep or too subtle for Strauss—unless it be granted that cynicism is more a part of comedy than a part of refined-insult. Let us also remember that Mr. Disston, not Mr. Strauss, put the funny notes in the bassoon. A symphony written only to amuse and entertain is likely to amuse only the writer—and him not long after the check is cashed.

"Genius is always ascetic and piety and love," thus Emerson reinforces "God's offer of this choice" by a transcendental definition. The moment a famous violinist refused "to appear" until he had received his check,—at that moment, *precisely* (assuming for argument's sake, that this was the first time that materialism had the ascendancy in this man's soul) at that moment he became but a man of "talent"—incidentally, a small man and a small violinist, regardless of how perfectly he played, regardless to what heights of emotion he stirred his audience, regardless of the sublimity of his artistic and financial success.

d'Annunzio, it is told, becoming somewhat discouraged at the result of some of his Fiume adventures said: "We are the only Idealists left." This remark may have been made in a moment of careless impulse, but if it is taken at its face value, the moment it was made that moment his idealism started downhill. A grasp at monopoly indicates that a sudden shift has taken place from the heights where genius may be found, to the lower plains of talent. The mind of a true idealist is great enough to know that a monopoly of idealism or of wheat is a thing nature does not support.

A newspaper music column prints an incident (so how can we assume that it is not true?) of an American violinist who called on Max Reger, to tell him how much he (the American) appreciated his music. Reger gives him a hopeless look and cries: "What! a musician and not speak German!" At that moment, by the clock, regardless of how great a genius he may have been before that sentence was uttered—at that moment he became but a man of "talent." "For the man of talent affects to call his transgressions of the laws of sense trivial and to count them nothing considered with his devotion to his art." His art never taught him prejudice or to wear only one eye. "His art is less for every deduction from his holiness and less for every defect of common sense." And this common sense has a great deal to do with this distinguishing difference of Emerson's between genius and talent, repose and truth, and between all evidences of substance and manner in art. Manner breeds partialists. "Is America a musical nation?"—if the man who is ever asking this question would sit down and think something over he might find less interest in asking it—he might possibly remember that all nations are more musical than any nation, especially the nation that pays the most—and pays the most eagerly, for anything, after it has been professionally—rubber-stamped. Music may be yet unborn. Perhaps no music has ever been written or heard. Perhaps the birth of art will take place at the moment, in which the last man, who is willing to make a living out of art is gone and gone forever. In the history of this youthful world the best product that human-beings can boast of is probably, Beethoven—but, maybe, even his art is as nothing in comparison with the future product of some coal-miner's soul in the forty-first century. And the same man who is ever asking about the most musical nation, is ever discovering the most musical man of the most musical nation. When particularly hysterical he shouts, "I have found him! Smith Grabholz—the one great American poet,—at last, here is the Moses the country has been waiting for"—(of course we all know that the country has not been waiting for anybody—and we have many Moses always with us). But the discoverer keeps right on shouting "Here is the one true American poetry, I pronounce it the work of a genius. I predict for him the most brilliant career—for *his* is an art that...—for *his* is a soul that ... for *his* is a..." and Grabholz is ruined;—but ruined, not alone, by this perennial discoverer of pearls in any oyster-shell that treats him the best, but ruined by his own (Grabholz's) talent,—for genius will never let itself be discovered by "a man." Then the world may ask "Can the one true national "this" or "that" be killed by its own discoverer?" "No," the country replies, "but each discovery is proof of another impossibility." It is a sad fact that the one true man and the one true art will never behave as they should except in the mind of the partialist whom God has forgotten. But this matters little to him (the man)—his business is good—for it is easy to sell the future in terms of the past—and there are always some who will buy anything. The individual usually *"gains"* if he is willing to but lean on "manner." The evidence of this is quite widespread, for if the discoverer happens to be in any other line of business his sudden discoveries would be just as important—*to him*. In fact, the theory of substance and manner in art and its related dualisms, "repose and truth, genius and talent," &c., may find illustration in many, perhaps most, of the human activities. And when examined it (the illustration) is quite likely to show how "manner" is always discovering partisans. For example, enthusiastic discoveries of the "paragon" are common in politics—an art to some. These revelations, in this profession are made easy by the pre-election discovering-leaders of the people. And the genius who is discovered, forthwith starts his speeches of "talent"—though they are hardly that—they are hardly more than a string of subplatitudes, square-looking, well-rigged things that almost everybody has seen, known, and heard since Rome or man fell. Nevertheless these signs of perfect manner, these series of noble sentiments that the "noble" never get off, are forcibly, clearly, and persuasively handed out—eloquently, even beautifully expressed, and with such personal charm, magnetism, and strength, that their profound messages speed right through the minds and hearts, without as much as spattering the walls, and land right square in the middle of the listener's vanity. For all this is a part of manner and its quality is of splendor—for manner is at times a good bluff but substance a poor one and knows it. The discovered one's usual and first great outburst is probably the greatest truth that he ever utters. Fearlessly standing, he looks straight into the eyes of the populace and with a strong ringing voice (for strong voices and strong statesmanship are inseparable) and with words far more eloquent than the following, he sings "This honor is greater than I deserve but duty calls me—(what, not stated) ... If elected, I shall be your servant" ... (for, it is told, that he believes in modesty,—that he has even boasted that he is the most modest man in the country)... Thus he has the right to shout, "First, last and forever I am for the people. I am against all bosses. I have no sympathy for politicians. I am for strict economy, liberal improvements and justice! I am also for the—ten commandments" (his intuitive political sagacity keeps him from mentioning any particular one).—But a sublime height is always reached in his perorations. Here we learn that he believes in *honesty*—(repeat *"honesty"*);—we are even allowed to infer that he is one of the very few who know that there is such a thing; and we also learn that since he was a little boy (barefoot) his motto has been "Do

Right,"—he swerves not from the right!—he believes in nothing but the right; (to him—everything is right!—if it gets him elected); but cheers invariably stop this great final truth (in brackets) from rising to animate expression. Now all of these translucent axioms are true (are not axioms always true?),—as far as manner is concerned. In other words, the manner functions perfectly. But where is the divine substance? This is not there—why should it be—if it were *he* might not be there. "Substance" is not featured in this discovery. For the truth of substance is sometimes silence, sometimes ellipses,—and the latter if supplied might turn some of the declarations above into perfect truths,—for instance "first and last and forever I am for the people ('s votes). I'm against all bosses (against me). I have no sympathy for (rival) politicians," etc., etc. But these tedious attempts at comedy should stop,—they're too serious,—besides the illustration may be a little hard on a few, the minority (the non-people) though not on the many, the majority (the people)! But even an assumed parody may help to show what a power manner is for reaction unless it is counterbalanced and then saturated by the other part of the duality. Thus it appears that all there is to this great discovery is that one good politician has discovered another good politician. For manner has brought forth its usual talent;—for manner cannot discover the genius who has discarded platitudes—the genius who has devised a new and surpassing order for mankind, simple and intricate enough, abstract and definite enough, locally impractical and universally practical enough, to wipe out the need for further discoveries of "talent" and incidentally the discoverer's own fortune and political "manner." Furthermore, he (this genius) never will be discovered until the majority-spirit, the common-heart, the human-oversoul, the source of all great values, converts all talent into genius, all manner into substance—until the direct expression of the mind and soul of the majority, the divine right of all consciousness, social, moral, and spiritual, discloses the one true art and thus finally discovers the one true leader—even *itself*:—then no leaders, no politicians, no manner, will hold sway—and no more speeches will be heard.

The intensity today, with which techniques and media are organized and used, tends to throw the mind away from a "common sense" and towards "manner" and thus to resultant weak and mental states—for example, the Byronic fallacy—that one who is full of turbid feeling *about himself* is qualified to be some sort of an artist. In this relation "manner" also leads some to think that emotional sympathy for self is as true a part of art as sympathy for others; and a prejudice in favor of the good and bad of one personality against the virtue of many personalities. It may be that when a poet or a whistler becomes conscious that he is in the easy path of any particular idiom,—that he is helplessly prejudiced in favor of any particular means of expression,—that his manner can be catalogued as modern or classic,—that he favors a contrapuntal groove, a sound-coloring one, a sensuous one, a successful one, or a melodious one (whatever that means),—that his interests lie in the French school or the German school, or the school of Saturn,—that he is involved in this particular "that" or that particular "this," or in any particular brand of emotional complexes,—in a word, when he becomes conscious that his style is "his personal own,"—that it has monopolized a geographical part of the world's sensibilities, then it may be that the value of his substance is not growing,—that it even may have started on its way backwards,—it may be that he is trading an inspiration for a bad habit and finally that he is reaching fame, permanence, or some other under-value, and that he is getting farther and farther from a perfect truth. But, on the contrary side of the picture, it is not unreasonable to imagine that if he (this poet, composer, and laborer) is open to all the overvalues within his reach,—if he stands unprotected from all the showers of the absolute which may beat upon him,—if he is willing to use or learn to use, or at least if he is not afraid of trying to use, whatever he can, of any and all lessons of the infinite that humanity has received and thrown to man,—that nature has exposed and sacrificed, that life and death have translated—if he accepts all and sympathizes with all, is influenced by all, whether consciously or subconsciously, drastically or humbly, audibly or inaudibly, whether it be all the virtue of Satan or the only evil of Heaven—and all, even, at one time, even in one chord,—*then* it may be that the value of his substance, and its value to himself, to his art, to all art, even to the Common Soul is growing and approaching nearer and nearer to perfect truths—whatever they are and wherever they may be.

Again, a certain kind of manner-over-influence may be caused by a group-disease germ. The over-influence by, the over-admiration of, and the over-association with a particular artistic personality or a particular type or group of personalities tends to produce equally favorable and unfavorable symptoms, but the unfavorable ones seem to be more contagious. Perhaps the impulse remark of some famous man (whose name we forget) that he "loved music but hated musicians," might be followed (with some good results) at least part of the time. To see the sun rise, a man has but to get up early, and he can always have Bach in his pocket. We hear that Mr. Smith or Mr. Morgan, etc., et al. design to establish a "course at Rome," to raise the standard of American music, (or the standard of American composers—which is it?) but possibly the more our composer accepts from his patrons *"et al."* the less he will accept *from himself.* It may be possible that a day in a "Kansas wheat field" will do more for him than three years in Rome. It may be, that many men—perhaps some of genius—(if you won't admit that all are geniuses) have been started on the downward path of subsidy by trying to write a thousand dollar prize poem or a ten thousand dollar prize opera. How many masterpieces have been prevented from blossoming in this way? A cocktail will make a man eat more, but will not give him a healthy, normal appetite (if he had not that already). If a bishop should offer a "prize living" to the curate who will love God the hardest for fifteen days, whoever gets the prize would love God the least. Such stimulants, it strikes us, tend to industrialize art, rather than develop a spiritual sturdiness—a sturdiness which Mr. Sedgwick says* "shows itself in a close union between spiritual life and the ordinary business of life," against spiritual feebleness which "shows itself in the separation of the two." If one's spiritual sturdiness is congenital and somewhat perfect he is not only conscious that this separation has no part in his own soul, but he does not feel its existence in others. He does not believe there is such a thing. But perfection in this respect is rare. And for the most of us, we believe, this sturdiness would be encouraged by anything that will keep or help us keep a normal balance between the spiritual life and the ordinary life. If for every thousand dollar prize a potato field be substituted, so that these candidates of "Clio" can dig a little in real life, perhaps dig up a natural inspiration, arts—air might be a little clearer—a little freer from certain traditional delusions, for instance, that free thought and free love always go to the same café—that atmosphere and diligence are synonymous. To quote Thoreau incorrectly: "When half-Gods talk, the Gods walk!" Everyone should have the opportunity of not being over-influenced.

Again, this over-influence by and over-insistence upon "manner" may finally lead some to believe "that manner for manner's sake is a basis of music." Someone is quoted as saying that "ragtime is the true American music." Anyone will admit that it is one of the many true, natural, and, nowadays, conventional means of expression. It is an idiom, perhaps a "set or series of colloquialisms," similar to those that have added through centuries and through natural means, some beauty to all languages. Every language is but the evolution of slang, and possibly the broad "A" in Harvard may have come down from the "butcher of Southwark." To examine ragtime rhythms and the syncopations of Schumann or of Brahms seems to the writer to show how much alike they are not. Ragtime, as we hear it, is, of course, more (but not much more) than a natural dogma of shifted accents, or a mixture of shifted and minus accents. It is something like wearing a derby hat on the back of the head, a shuffling lilt of a happy soul just let out of a Baptist Church in old Alabama. Ragtime has its possibilities. But it does not "represent the American nation" any more than some fine old senators represent it. Perhaps we know it now as an ore before it has been refined into a product. It may be one of nature's ways of giving art raw material. Time will throw its vices away and weld its virtues into the fabric of our music. It has its uses as the cruet on the boarding-house table has, but to make a meal of tomato ketchup and horse-radish, to plant a whole farm with sunflowers, even to put a sunflower into every bouquet, would be calling nature something worse than a politician. Mr. Daniel Gregory Mason, whose wholesome influence, by the way, is doing as much perhaps for music in America as American music is, amusingly says: "If indeed the land of Lincoln and Emerson has degenerated until nothing remains of it but a 'jerk and rattle,' then we, at least, are free to repudiate this false patriotism of 'my Country right or wrong,' to insist that better than bad music is no music, and to let our beloved art subside finally under the clangor of the subway gongs and automobile horns, dead, but not dishonored." And so may we ask: Is it better to sing inadequately of the "leaf on Walden floating," and die "dead but not dishonored," or to sing adequately of the "cherry on the cocktail," and live forever?

6

If anyone has been strong enough to escape these rocks—this "Scylla and Charybdis,"—has survived these wrong choices, these under-values with their prizes, Bohemias and heroes, is not such a one in a better position, is he not abler and freer to "declare himself and so to love his cause so singly that he will cleave to it, and forsake all else? What is this cause for the American composer but the utmost musical beauty that he, as an individual man, with his own qualities and defects, is capable of understanding and striving towards?—forsaking all else except those types of musical beauty that come home to him,"* and that his spiritual conscience intuitively approves.

"It matters not one jot, provided this course of personal loyalty to a cause be steadfastly pursued, what the special characteristics of the style of the music may be to which one gives one's devotion."* This, if over-translated, may be made to mean, what we have been trying to say—that if your interest, enthusiasm, and devotion on the side of substance and truth, are of the stuff to make you so sincere that you sweat—to hell with manner and repose! Mr. Mason is responsible for too many young minds, in their planting season to talk like this, to be as rough, or to go as far, but he would probably admit that, broadly speaking—some such way, *i.e.*, constantly recognizing this ideal duality in art, though not the most profitable road for art to travel, is almost its only way out to eventual freedom and salvation. Sidney Lanier, in a letter to Bayard Taylor writes: "I have so many fair dreams and hopes about music in these days (1875). It is gospel whereof the people are in great need. As Christ gathered up the Ten Commandments and redistilled them into the clear liquid of the wondrous

---

* John C. Griggs, "Debussy" Yale Review, 1914.

* Contemporary Composers, D. G. Mason, Macmillan Co., N.Y.
* *Ibid.*

eleventh—love God utterly and thy neighbor as thyself—so I think the time will come when music *rightly developed* to its now little foreseen *grandeur* will be found to be a late revelation of all gospels in one." Could the art of music, or the art of anything have a more profound reason for being than this? A conception unlimited by the narrow names of Christian, Pagan, Jew, or Angel! A vision higher and deeper than art itself!

7

The humblest composer will not find true humility in aiming low—he must never be timid or afraid of trying to express that which he feels is far above his power to express, any more than he should be afraid of breaking away, when necessary, from easy first sounds, or afraid of admitting that those half truths that come to him at rare intervals, are half true, for instance, that all art galleries contain masterpieces, which are nothing more than a history of art's beautiful mistakes. He should never fear of being called a highbrow—but not the kind in Prof. Brander Matthews' definition. John L. Sullivan was a "high-brow" in his art. A high-brow can always whip a low-brow.

If he "truly seeks," he "will surely find" many things to sustain him. He can go to a part of Alcott's philosophy—"that all occupations of man's body and soul in their diversity come from but one mind and soul!" If he feels that to subscribe to all of the foregoing and then submit, though not as evidence, the work of his own hands is presumptuous, let him remember that a man is not always responsible for the wart on his face, or a girl for the bloom on her cheek, and as they walk out of a Sunday for an airing, people will see them—but they must have the air. He can remember with Plotinus, "that in every human soul there is the ray of the celestial beauty," and therefore every human outburst may contain a partial ray. And he can believe that it is better to go to the plate and strike out than to hold the bench down, for by facing the pitcher, he may then know the umpire better, and possibly see a new parabola. His presumption, if it be that, may be but a kind of courage juvenal sings about, and no harm can then be done either side. *"Cantabit vacuus coram latrone viator."*

8

To divide by an arbitrary line something that cannot be divided is a process that is disturbing to some. Perhaps our deductions are not as inevitable as they are logical, which suggests that they are not "logic." An arbitrary assumption is never fair to all any of the time, or to anyone all the time. Many will resent the abrupt separation that a theory of duality in music suggests and say that these general subdivisions are too closely inter-related to be labeled decisively— "this or that." There is justice in this criticism, but our answer is that it is better to be short on the long than long on the short. In such an abstruse art as music it is easy for one to point to this as substance and to that as manner. Some will hold and it is undeniable—in fact quite obvious—that manner has a great deal to do with the beauty of substance, and that to make a too arbitrary division, or distinction between them, is to interfere, to some extent, with an art's beauty and unity. There is a great deal of truth in this too. But on the other hand, beauty in music is too often confused with something that lets the ears lie back in an easy chair. Many sounds that we are used to, do not bother us, and for that reason, we are inclined to call them beautiful. Frequently,—possibly almost invariably,—analytical and impersonal tests will show, we believe, that when a new or unfamiliar work is accepted as beautiful on its first hearing, its fundamental quality is one that tends to put the mind to sleep. A narcotic is not always unnecessary, but it is seldom a basis of progress,—that is, wholesome evolution in any creative experience. This kind of progress has a great deal to do with beauty—at least in its deeper emotional interests, if not in its moral values. (The above is only a personal impression, but it is based on carefully remembered instances, during a period of about fifteen or twenty years.) Possibly the fondness for individual utterance may throw out a skin-deep arrangement, which is readily accepted as beautiful—formulæ that weaken rather than toughen up the musical-muscles. If the composer's sincere conception of his art and of its functions and ideals, coincide to such an extent with these groove-colored permutations of tried out progressions in expediency, that he can arrange them over and over again to his transcendent delight—has he or has he not been drugged with an overdose of habit-forming sounds? And as a result do not the muscles of his clientele become flabbier and flabbier until they give way altogether and find refuge only in a seasoned opera box—where they can see without thinking? And unity is too generally conceived of, or too easily accepted as analogous to form, and form (as analogous) to custom, and custom to habit, and habit may be one of the parents of custom and form, and there are all kinds of parents. Perhaps all unity in art, at its inception, is half-natural and half-artificial but time insists, or at least makes us, or inclines to make us feel that it is all natural. It is easy for us to accept it as such. The "unity of dress" for a man at a ball requires a collar, yet he could dance better without it. Coherence, to a certain extent, must bear some relation to the listener's subconscious perspective. For example, a critic has to listen to a thousand concerts a year, in which there is much repetition, not only of the same pieces, but the same formal relations of tones, cadences, progressions, etc. There is present a certain routine series of image-necessity-stimulants, which he doesn't seem to need until they disappear. Instead of listening to music, he listens around it. And from this subconscious viewpoint, he inclines perhaps more to the thinking about than thinking in music. If he could go into some other line of business for a year or so perhaps his perspective would be more naturally normal. The unity of a sonata movement has long been associated with its form, and to a greater extent than is necessary. A first theme, a development, a second in a related key and its development, the free fantasia, the recapitulation, and so on, and over again. Mr. Richter or Mr. Parker may tell us that all this is natural, for it is based on the classic-song form, but in spite of your teachers a vague feeling sometimes creeps over you that the form-nature of the song has been stretched out into deformity. Some claim for Tchaikowsky that his clarity and coherence of design is unparalleled (or some such word) in works for the orchestra. That depends, it seems to us, on how far repetition is an essential part of clarity and coherence. We know that butter comes from cream—but how long must we watch the "churning arm!" If nature is not enthusiastic about explanation, why should Tschaikowsky be? Beethoven had to churn, to some extent, to make his message carry. He had to pull the ear, hard and in the same place and several times, for the 1790 ear was tougher than the 1890 one. But the "great Russian weeper" might have spared us. To Emerson, "unity and the over-soul, or the common-heart, are synonymous." Unity is at least nearer to these than to solid geometry, though geometry may be all unity.

But to whatever unpleasantness the holding to this theory of duality brings us, we feel that there is a natural law underneath it all, and like all laws of nature, a liberal interpretation is the one nearest the truth. What part of these supplements are opposites? What part of substance is manner? What part of this duality is polarity? These questions though not immaterial may be disregarded, if there be a sincere appreciation (intuition is always sincere) of the "divine" spirit of the thing. Enthusiasm for, and recognition of these higher over these lower values will transform a destructive iconoclasm into creation, and a mere devotion into consecration—a consecration which, like Amphion's music, will raise the Walls of Thebes.

9

Assuming, and then granting, that art-activity can be transformed or led towards an eventual consecration, by recognizing and using in their true relation, as much as one can, these higher and lower dual values—and that the doing so is a part, if not the whole of our old problem of paralleling or approving in art the highest attributes, moral and spiritual, one sees in life—if you will grant all this, let us offer a practical suggestion—a thing that one who has imposed the foregoing should try to do just out of common decency, though it be but an attempt, perhaps, to make his speculations less speculative, and to beat off metaphysics.

All, men-bards with a divine spark, and bards without, feel the need at times of an inspiration from without, "the breath of another soul to stir our inner flame," especially when we are in pursuit of a part of that "utmost musical beauty," that we are capable of understanding—when we are breathlessly running to catch a glimpse of that unforeseen grandeur of Mr. Lanier's dream. In this beauty and grandeur perhaps marionettes and their souls have a part—though how great their part is, we hear, is still undetermined; but it is morally certain that, at times, a part with itself must be some of those greater contemplations that have been caught in the "World's Soul," as it were, and nourished for us there in the soil of its literature.

If an interest in, and a sympathy for, the thought-visions of men like Charles Kingsley, Marcus Aurelius, Whittier, Montaigne, Paul of Tarsus, Robert Browning, Pythagoras, Channing, Milton, Sophocles, Swedenborg, Thoreau, Francis of Assisi, Wordsworth, Voltaire, Garrison, Plutarch, Ruskin, Ariosto, and all kindred spirits and souls of great measure, from David down to Rupert Brooke,—if a study of the thought of such men creates a sympathy, even a love for them and their ideal-part, it is certain that this, however inadequately expressed, is nearer to what music was given man for, than a devotion to "Tristan's sensual love of Isolde," to the "Tragic Murder of a Drunken Duke," or to the sad thoughts of a bathtub when the water is being let out. It matters little here whether a man who paints a picture of a useless beautiful landscape *imperfectly* is a greater genius than the man who paints a useful bad smell *perfectly.*

It is not intended in this suggestion that inspirations coming from the higher planes should be limited to any particular thought or work, as the mind receives it. The plan rather embraces all that should go with an expression of the composite-value. It is of the underlying spirit, the direct unrestricted imprint of one soul on another, a portrait, not a photograph of the personality—it is the ideal part that would be caught in this canvas. It is a sympathy for "substance"—the over-value together with a consciousness that there must be a lower value—the "Demosthenic part of the Philippics"—the "Ciceronic part of the Catiline," the sublimity, against the vileness of Rousseau's *Confessions*. It is something akin to, but something more than these predominant partial tones of Hawthorne—"the grand old countenance of Homer; the decrepit form, but vivid face of Aesop; the dark presence of Dante; the wild Ariosto; Rabelais' smile of deep-wrought mirth; the profound, pathetic humor of Cervantes; the all-glorious Shakespeare; Spenser, meet guest for allegoric structure; the severe divinity of Milton; and Bunyan, molded of humblest clay, but instinct with celestial fire."

There are communities now, partly vanished, but cherished and sacred, scattered throughout this world of ours, in which freedom of thought and soul, and even of body, have been fought for. And we believe that there ever lives in that part of the over-soul, native to them, the thoughts which these freedom-struggles have inspired. America is not too young to have its divinities, and its place legends. Many of those "Transcendent Thoughts" and "Visions" which had their birth beneath our Concord elms—messages that have brought salvation to many listening souls throughout the world—are still growing, day by day, to greater and greater beauty—are still showing clearer and clearer man's way to God!

No true composer will take his substance from another finite being—but there are times, when he feels that his self-expression needs some liberation from at least a part of his own soul. At such times, shall he not better turn to those greater souls, rather than to the external, the immediate, and the "Garish Day"?

The strains of one man may fall far below the course of those Phaetons of Concord, or of the Ægean Sea, or of Westmorland—but the greater the distance his music falls away, the more reason that some greater man shall bring his nearer those higher spheres.

PIANO SONATA NO. 2
CONCORD

CONTENTS

I. "Emerson"   4
II. "Hawthorne"   22
III. "The Alcotts"   52
IV. "Thoreau"   57

I. "Emerson"

Note:— As a general rule, the notes are natural, unless otherwise marked, except those immediately following a note with an accidental,— natural signs are thus used more as a convenience than of necessity.

(Throughout this and the other movements, there are many chords, the notes of which obviously cannot be struck together, though the roll or arpeggio mark is not used.)

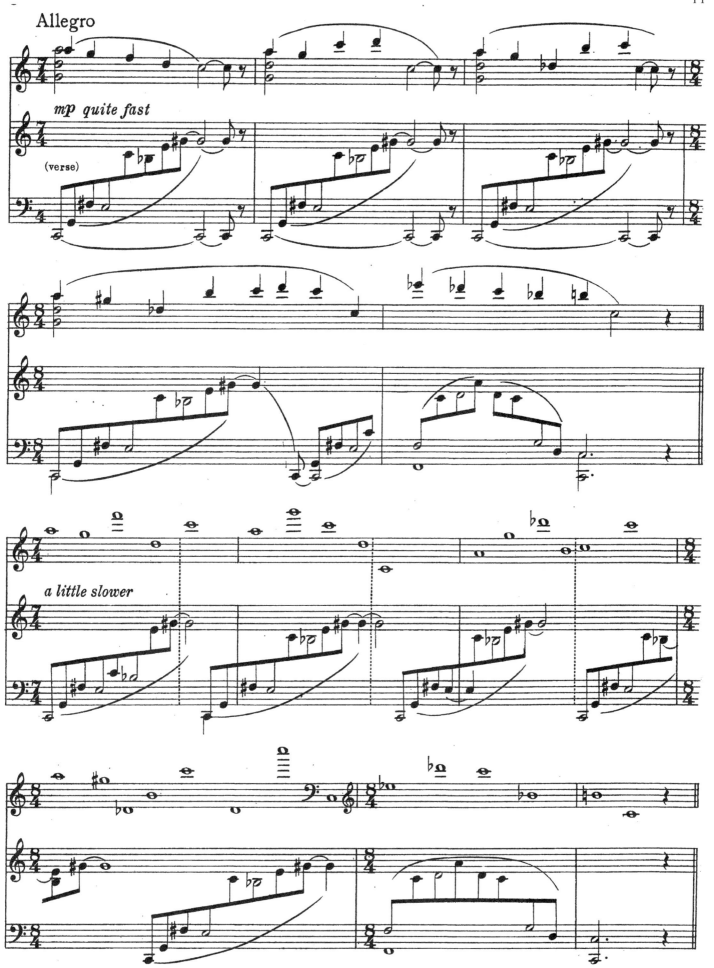

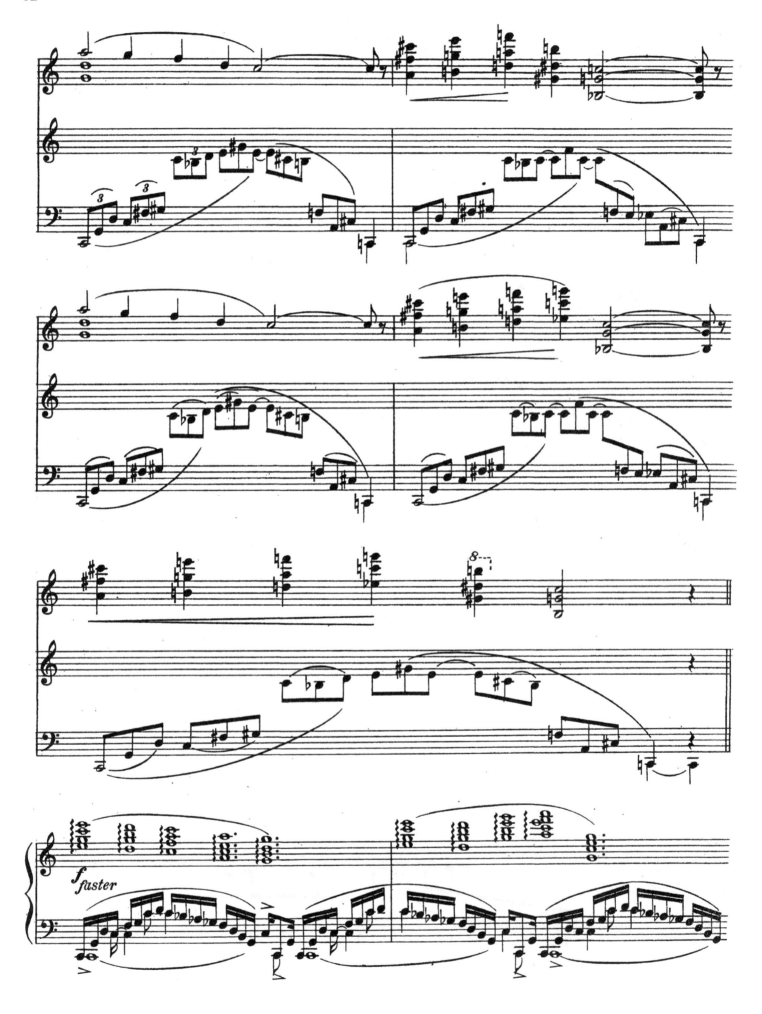

*) To be heard as a kind of an overtone

II. "Hawthorne"

1. For the most part, this movement is supposed to be played as fast as possible, lightly and not literally. Marks of tempo, expression, etc. are use as little as possible. If the score itself, the preface or an interest in Hawthorne suggest nothing, marks will only make things worse. 2 It is not intended that the relation 2:1. between the 32nd & 16th notes here, be held to literally, 3. The use of both pedals is almost constantly required.

24

26

*Played by using a strip of board 14¾ ins. long and heavy enough to press the keys down without striking.

31

42

45

III. "The Alcotts"

IV. "Thoreau"

* This Thoreau movement, is supposed to be played in a lower dynamic ratio than usual;- i.e, the "forte" here is about the "mezzo piano" of the preceding movements.
Both pedals are used almost constantly.

*Small notes in piano to be played only if flute is not used.